The Old Man's Reader

Old Man by Moonlight—Reassuring in the Silent Glow of Moon and Stars. From *The Old Man and His Dream* by Charles G. Chase. Illustrations by D.T.K. as reproduced in *The Franconia Gateway* by G. Waldo Browne. From the author's collection.

The Old Man's Reader

History & Legends of
Franconia Notch

Compiled and Edited
by
John T. B. Mudge

The Durand Press
Etna, New Hampshire

ISBN 0-9633560-3-8

Printed in the United States of America by BookCrafters. Typesetting and design by LaserLab, Hanover, New Hampshire 03755. The text of this book is set in Adobe, Inc.'s Stempel Garamond.

Publication history: First Edition 1995
Imprint is last number shown: 9 8 7 6 5 4 3 2 1

Dedication

Throughout the history of the White Mountains many individuals and groups have worked to preserve the beauty and history of that region of New Hampshire. This book is dedicated to all of those persons and organizations whose foresight and energy have been and continue to be dedicated to that cause. Could he speak, the Old Man of the Mountain would also be quietly saying, "Thank you."

Franconia! thy wild hills are dear to me,
Would their green woods might be my spirit's home.

Harry Hibbard

About the Author

John Mudge is a financial planner, a small business consultant and a writer about White Mountain history. He is the author of *The White Mountains: Names, Places and Legends* published in 1992 and *Mapping the White Mountains*, published in 1993. A graduate of the Northfield-Mount Hermon School, Amherst College, and the Whittemore School of Business and Economics at the University of New Hampshire, he is a member of the Appalachian Mountain Club, the Randolph Mountain Club, and the Society for the Protection of New Hampshire Forests. He has visited the White Mountains regularly for the past forty years and continues to visit and climb there as often as he can. Today he lives in Etna, New Hampshire.

Contents

THE GREAT STONE FACE

A PLAY AND POETRY

FINAL WORDS

Introduction

HIGH ABOVE the Franconia Notch gateway to northern New Hampshire there is an old man who is often visited by new friends and old acquaintances. Every visitor finds their host to be changeless, and each perhaps wonders aloud to a friend or quietly to themselves, "Who are you Old Man of the Mountain?"

The Old Man has been described as a relentless tyrant, a fantastic freak, and a learned philosopher, feeble and weak about the mouth and of rarest beauty, stern and solemn, one of the most remarkable wonders of the mountain world, and simply five granite ledges. While modern man has known the Old Man only since 1805, for unknown ages he has witnessed, survived, and been weathered by summer's heat and winter's cold, lightning and thunder, and rain, wind, and snow. He is a symbol of endurance. He is the emblem of the State of New Hampshire. His likeness has been used innumerable times as an advertising symbol for products as diverse as they are numerous.

While many millions of people have passed below the Old Man's silent gaze and responded with a passing glance and a few quick words to a friend, others have paused longer and written down their words about his countenance. This book is a collection of those writings. These are their thoughts about the Old Man, and these are the words and thoughts that they have sometimes attributed to the Old Man of the Mountain of Franconia Notch in the White Mountains of New Hampshire.

The primary purpose here is to provide the reader with a little more historical information and to introduce the different sections of the book. A few very preliminary words: First, wherever possible, each of the articles reprinted here is preceded by some biographical information about its author, some more extensive than others. Secondly, the name: The reader will soon discover that the Old Man of the Mountain has several names including "The Profile", "The Great Stone Face", "The Old Man," and *mountain* in the plural, "The Old Man of the Mountains." Please accept all of these names just as a person might have several nicknames. The Old Man is never known to have expressed a preference, and this introduction, like the authors and writings that follow, will use the different names interchangeably. And lastly, The Profile is composed of Conway red granite and is an illusion formed by five ledges, that when lined up correctly give the appearance of an old man with an easterly gaze, clearly distinct and visible from only a very small space near Profile Lake. When viewed from other locations in Franconia Notch, the same five ledges have a very rough and ragged appearance, and there is no suggestion of The Profile. The Old Man has been measured as being forty feet and five inches in height and 1,200 feet above Profile Lake.

This book contains the writings of thirty-eight men and women. A president, a governor, a congressman, a teacher, and a minister are but a few of the people who have paused to write about the Old Man of the Mountain since he was first seen nearly two centuries ago. Undoubtedly there exist other writings, literary and historical, about the Old Man of the Mountain. A story or poem may have appeared only once in a now forgotten and out-of-print newspaper. A far away visitor may have written a short story for publication in their hometown newspaper, and another visitor may have written down their very personal thoughts and secured them in the privacy of their desk. The readings selected for this book are in their entirety about the Old Man and his home in Franconia Notch. A poem about the White Mountains that included only a single line or verse about the most distinguished resident of Franconia Notch would have been purposely excluded from this collection. The writings that are not here may be no less important than the material that is in this book, and perhaps someday all of these writings will be collected together.

The first section of the book, *Setting the Scene*, reprints the works of two ornithologists. Their words can only begin to capture the essence of the notch, but they do take us into the notch for the rest of the readings.

The second section of the book contains three Indian legends. From a modern historical point of view, The Profile was first seen in 1805. There is no archeological or other evidence that the nomadic hunters who came to northern New Hampshire after the last ice age, over 10,000 years ago, or their successors, the Abenaki Indians, knew about or in any manner visited or had any religious or ceremonial association with what the white settlers first saw in 1805. The Indian legends that exist must be accepted as that, legends, stories to be enjoyed by modern readers.

With the growing tourist industry in northern New Hampshire at the end of the nineteenth century there was an ever increasing demand for guidebooks and histories of the region. The fourth section of this book reprints material about the Old Man from these different publications. Different writers have attributed the discovery of 1805 to either Nathaniel Hall of Thornton, New Hampshire, or to Luke Brooks and Francis Whitcomb, both of Franconia, New Hampshire. Working separately, these two parties reportedly looked with amazement at the profile above them. Hall, awed by his discovery, forgot about the birds that he was hunting and rushed back to tell his fellow workers. Responding with equal surprise and amazement at their independent discovery, Brooks and Whitcomb reportedly exclaimed, "That is Jefferson," he then being the President of the young United States. And since that time, the Old Man of the Mountains has had many friends, including those whose writings are reprinted here.

As he has silently gazed down upon Franconia Notch and to the White Mountains to the east, the Old Man has seen ox carts, stage coaches, and the modern interstate system pass below him as northern New Hampshire has been developed and commerce has flowed to and from the White Mountains. For many years the center of this commerce in Franconia Notch was a hotel, The Profile House. Contemporary visitors to Franconia Notch, while standing in the parking lot beside the modern tramway, may find it difficult to imagine the grand splendor of the Profile House that previously occupied this site and is described in the fifth section of the book. The first Profile House was constructed by Richard Taft in 1852 and had 110 rooms. In 1857 Charles Greenleaf began a long career with the hotel when he first worked there as a bell-boy. Greenleaf returned to work at the hotel for several summers until 1865 when he became a member of the hotel company. After 1878, when the Profile and Franconia Notch Railroad Company constructed a narrow gauge railroad between the town of Bethlehem and the Profile House, two engines, *The Profile* and *The Echo*, regularly pulled a train consisting of one passenger car and one baggage car during the busy summer months. Charles Greenleaf became the sole proprietor of the hotel in 1881 when Richard Taft died. By the fall of 1905 the increased demands on the hotel caused Greenleaf to tear down the original building, and through the following winter the workmen built a new hotel with 400 rooms and a dining room that could seat 600 guests. By the following summer all of the work was completed and the hotel was open. Perhaps the most memorable entertainment ever performed at the hotel was the evening that P. T. Barnum dressed the employees as animals, and they performed a circus for the guests. In the fall of 1920, with the increasing popularity of the automobile, *The Profile* and *The Echo* made their last trips out of Franconia Notch. Upon retirement in 1921 Greenleaf sold his hotel to the company of Frank Abbott and Son, innkeepers in Bethlehem, New Hampshire. Two years later, on August 3, 1923, the Profile House and all of the surrounding buildings were destroyed by a fire of unknown origins. Karl Abbott wrote:

> The entire entrance to the Notch was a blazing inferno against which the puny efforts of man were inconsequential. By the time I arrived our beautiful little mountain community was an area of smoldering ashes. A state of chaos prevailed in the ruined Notch.

An era had come to an end in Franconia Notch. The section of this book about the Profile House is but a small attempt to remember the hotel and the friends of the Old Man who visited there during that period.

After the 1923 fire the Abbott family decided not to rebuild a hotel in Franconia Notch. The land was for sale. Led by the Society for the Protection of New Hampshire Forests, the Old Man's friends responded and Franconia Notch State Park was created. The State of New Hampshire appropriated $200,000, James J. Storrow of Boston contributed $100,000 and over 15,000 other individuals and groups contributed the remaining $100,000 that resulted in the purchase and subsequent public ownership of the land.

The seventh and eighth sections of the book contain a play and poetry that have been written about The Profile. The diversity of these pieces is very great. Some readers may think that the longer poems should have been edited, but in an effort to preserve both intellectual honesty and the original style and intent of the authors no such editing has been done. The *Three Impressions* near the end of this book are very different pieces from a Swedish novelist, an American President and a Constitutional lawyer. (Astute readers will have noted that the third and sixth sections have not yet been mentioned. Those sections reprint, in their entirety, two very different and popular works about The Old Man.) And lastly, in an effort to engage in participatory literature readers of this book are invited to complete the epilogue.

The Old Man has had many friends who have cared for him at different times. In the 1870's a group from the Appalachian Mountain Club reported that a stone on his forehead was in danger of falling off. This observation was forgotten until 1916 when the Reverend Guy Roberts of Whitefield, New Hampshire, climbed up the mountain and reported the same observation to Charles Greenleaf the proprietor of the Profile House. In the fall of 1916 Edward H. Geddes performed the first repairs, the installation of three sets of anchor irons each weighing 450 pounds, on the Old Man of the Mountain. The Old

Man was beginning to be tied together so that he would not fall into the notch below. In 1965 Niels F. Nielsen of Plymouth, New Hampshire, became the Old Man's caretaker, and that responsibility has now been assumed by his son, David Nielsen of Gilmanton, New Hampshire. Today the regular inspections keep the turnbuckles maintained, the epoxy and fiberglass properly applied, and The Profile hopefully secure. Born in the melting glaciers and silently formed by the hands of time, the Old Man of the Mountains is as safe today as his friends can make him.

Perhaps the greatest controversy that has ever involved the Old Man was the construction of the interstate highway through Franconia Notch when his friends were strongly opposed to the building of a four lane highway. In 1979, after nearly two decades of controversy, Congressman James Cleveland and his staff developed a compromise plan, and a restricted access parkway was built. Just as the highway controversy had a happy ending so did a 1955 children's story, *Larry Tours Franconia Notch New Hampshire* by Lula Shaver, which described the family car trip through the notch:

> As they neared Profile Mountain where the Old Stone Face kept vigil over his beloved State of New Hampshire, Larry's Dad drove slowly so the young lad wouldn't miss the breath-taking moment when the Old Man of the Mountains came into full view.
>
> Suddenly, he was there, his kind face gazing calmly over the countryside. Larry stared at the Great Profile in solemn wonder and said, "There he is, Dad!" Like everyone else Larry felt awed by the sight.

Hopefully today's children of all ages will experience the same excitement and fun as they travel through Franconia Notch and the White Mountains.

❖ ❖ ❖

1939 postcard. From the author's collection.

As I researched and prepared this book I was fortunate to have assistance and suggestions from a large number of people and institutions. My work would have been much more difficult without all of that help. I am indebted to the staff of the New Hampshire Historical Society and the Historical Society of Pennsylvania for their assistance in researching several very specific and obscure items. The contents of this book would be incomplete without the rare books that several antiquarian booksellers in New Hampshire found for me. Those booksellers were: Broadway Books of Derry, Village Books of Rumney, Titles and Tales of Littleton, and Sykes and Flanders of Weare. I am grateful to the Dwight D. Eisenhower Library of Abilene, Kansas, for its assistance in obtaining a copy of President Eisenhower's speech. The Christian Science Church of Boston assisted in the publication of the poem by Mary Baker Eddy. Chris Brooks and the Franconia Area Heritage Council put me in contact with Eleanor R. Lovett of Franconia, New Hampshire, who kindly provided me with information about the play that is reprinted here. As in past projects, LaserLab of Hanover, New Hampshire, played an indispensable role in the design of the book. And lastly, I had a great deal of assistance from the Research Desk, the Circulation Desk, and the Special Collections Department of the Dartmouth College Library. All students of the White Mountains should be grateful for the large collection of rare White Mountain materials that is safely housed but so readily available to all who come to use this library.

This is a book of many pieces and to fully enjoy the whole of the book, each of the little pieces must be read and enjoyed by itself. The book is not meant to be read through from cover to cover in a single evening. It should be read in parts, put down, and then returned to for another reading of another part. And after reading all of the "parts" of the book, in whatever order is most enjoyable, I believe that the reader will find that their enjoyment of the whole of the book has been greater than it would have been had the book been read from cover-to-cover.

Secondly, some readers may want to find an underlying theme in these writings. No effort has been made to incorporate any theme into the book other than just The Old Man of the Mountain himself. Similarly, no editorial effort has been made to compare the different references to the Indians, the religious characteristics that have been attributed to the Old Man, or to cross reference the different writers' own references to one another. Readers interested in such a study may find it an interesting exercise.

Lastly, there is the question of style and spelling. Some spelling rules and writing styles have been modified since these pieces were first written and published. This collection retains the authors' original spelling and style. And if after reading and completing the epilogue any readers have suggestions or contributions that they wish to make, those may be forwarded, regardless of style, to the publisher who will be very grateful for them.

John T. B. Mudge
Etna, New Hampshire.

January 1995

Early Days

Setting the Scene

Indian Legends

SETTING THE SCENE

Footing It in Franconia
Bradford Torrey

Bradford Torrey, 1843-1912, authored eight books on ornithology in different parts of the United States. One publication once wrote of Torrey: "He is entitled to high rank as a field ornithologist, which to this he adds a happy way of telling what he sees." *Footing It in Franconia*, published by Houghton Mifflin in 1901, contained both his recollections of the birds that he saw and heard and his other observations as a naturalist while visiting Franconia and Bethlehem at different seasons. Torrey uses both the names "Mount Cannon" and "Profile Mountain" but never in his book does he mention or describe "The Old Man of the Mountain."

AUTUMN

T IS TEN O'CLOCK. Slowly as I have come, not a wagonload of tourists has caught up with me; and at the Bald Mountain path I leave the highway, having a sudden notion to go to Echo Lake by the way of Artist's Bluff, so called, a rocky cliff that rises abruptly from the lower end of the lake. The trail conducts me through a veritable fernery, one long slope being thickly set with perfectly fresh shield-ferns—*Aspidium spinulosum* and perhaps *A. dilatatum,* though I do not concern myself to be sure of it. From the bluff the lake is at my feet, but what mostly fills my eye is the woods on the lower side of Mount Cannon. There is no language to express the kind of pleasure I take in them: so soft, so bright, so various in their hues,—dark green, light green, russet, yellow, red,—all drowned in sunshine, yet veiled perceptibly with haze even at this slight distance. If there is anything in nature more exquisitely, ravishingly beautiful than an old mountainside forest looked at from above, I do not know where to find it.

Down at the lakeside, there is beauty of another kind: The level blue water, the clean gray shallows about its margin, the reflections of bright mountains—Eagle Cliff and Mount Cannon—in its face, and soaring into the sky, on either side and in front, the mountains themselves. And how softly the ground is matted under the shrubbery and trees: twin-flower, partridge berry, creeping snowberry, gold-thread, oxalis, dwarf cornel, checkerberry, trailing arbutus! The very names ought to be a means of grace to the pen that writes them.… .

SPRING

…One of the principal glories of Franconia is the same in spring as in autumn,—the colors of the forest. There is no describing them: greens and reds of all tender and lovely shades; not to speak of the exquisite haze-blue, or blue-purple, which mantles the still budded woods on the higher slopes. For the reds I was quite unprepared. They have never been written about, so far as I know, doubtless because they have never been seen. The scribbling tourist is never here till long after they are gone. In fact, I stayed late enough, on my present visit, to see the end of them. I knew, of course, that young maple leaves, like old ones, are of a ruddy complexion; but somehow I had never considered that the massing of the trees on the hillsides

Echo Lake, New Hampshire. Jasper F. Cropsey, 1823-1900. Lithograph from the author's collection.

would work the same gorgeous, spectacular effect in spring as in autumn,—broad patches of splendor hung aloft, a natural tapestry, for the eye to feast upon. Not that May is as gaudy as September. There are no brilliant yellows, and the reds are many shades less fiery than autumn furnishes; but what is lacking in intensity is more than made up in delicacy, as the bloom of youth is fairer than any hectic flush... .

...Then, as I pass the height of land and begin the gentle descent into the Notch, fronting the white peak of Lafayette and the black face of Eagle Cliff, I am aware of a strange sensation, as if I had stepped into another world: bare, leafless woods and sudden blank silence. All the way hitherto birds have been singing on either hand, my ear picking out the voices one by one, while flies and mosquitoes have buzzed continually about my head: here, all in a moment, not a bird, not an insect,—stillness like that of winter. Minute after minute, rod after rod, and not a breath of sound, not so much as the stirring of a leaf. I could not have believed such a transformation possible. It is uncanny. I walk as in a dream. The silence lasts for at least a quarter of a mile. Then a warbler breaks it for an instant, and leaves it, if possible, more absolute than before. I am going southward, and downhill; but I am going into the Notch, into the very shadow of the mountains, where Winter makes his last rally against the inevitable.

A DAY IN JUNE

... it is nearly noon by the time I turn into the footpath that leads down to Echo Lake. Here the air is full of toad voices; a chorus of long-drawn trills in the shrillest of musical tones. If the creatures (the sandy shore and its immediate shallows are thick with them) are attempting to set up an echo, they meet with no success. At all events I hear no response, though the fault may easily be in my hearing, insusceptible as it is to vibrations above a certain pitch of fineness. What ethereal music it would be, an echo of toad trills from the grand sounding-board of Eagle Cliff! In the density of my ignorance I am surprised to find such numbers of these humble, half-domesticated, garden-loving batrachians congregated here in the wilderness. If the day were less mid-summery, and were not already mortgaged to other plans, I would go to Profile Lake to see whether the same thing is going on there. I should have looked upon these lovely sheets of mountain water as spawning places for trout. But toads!— that seems another matter. If I am surprised at their presence, however, they seem equally so at mine. And who knows? They were here first. Perhaps I am the intruder. I wish them no harm in any case. If black flies form any considerable part of their diet, they could not multiply too rapidly, though every note of trill were good for a polliwog, and every polliwog should grow into the portliest of toads.

BERRY-TIME FELICITIES

...I came to the burning, a tract of forest over which a fire had run some two years before. Here, in this dead place, there was more of life; more sunshine, and therefore more insects, and therefore more birds. Even here, however, there was nothing to be called birdiness: a few olive-sided flycatchers and wood pewees, both with musical whistles, one like a challenge, the other an elegy; a family group of chestnut-sided warblers, parents and young, conversing softly among themselves about the events of the day, mostly gastronomic, a robin and a white-throated sparrow in song; three or four chickadees, lisping and *deeing*; a siskin or two, a song sparrow, a red-eyed vireo. The whole tract was purple with willow herb—which follows fire as surely as boys follow a fire engine—and white with pearly immortelles.

Once out of this open space—this forest cemetery, one might say, though the dead were not buried, but stood upright like bleached skeletons, with arms outstretched—I was again immersed in leafy silence, which lasted till I approached the lake.

Here I heard before me the tweeting of sandpipers, and presently came in sight of two solitaries (migrants already, though it was only the 4th of August), each bobbing nervously upon its boulder a little off shore. The eye of the ornithologist took them in: dark green legs; dark, slender bills; bobbing, not teetering—*Totanus*, not *Actitis*. Then the eyes of the man turned to rest upon that enchanting prospect: Eagle Cliff in shadow, Profile Mountain in full sun, and the lake between them. The spirit of all the hours I had ever spent here was communing with me. I blessed the place and bade it good-by. "I will come again if I can," I said, "and many times; but if not, good-by." I believe I am like the birds; no matter how far south they may wander, when the winter is gone they say one to another, "Let us go back to the north country, to the place where we were so happy a year ago."

The Franconia Notch

Paul R. Jenks

The Granite Monthly regularly included history, biography, literature and other material about New Hampshire and its people. *The
Franconia Notch* by Paul R. Jenks was printed in August 1901. The
writings of Jenks and Bradford Torrey are similar and Jenks even
refers to Torrey's description of the colors of Franconia Notch in
May—springtime.

RE YOU familiar with the Franconia notch?" "Oh,
yes; I've been through it twice, and been another time
by railway to the Profile House and taken dinner there.
It's a great place, isn't it?"

Pretty much like this is American familiarity. I do not rep-
rehend it, for it bespeaks acquaintance with wide areas, and a
broad general knowledge that is admirable. Thoroughness is
indeed but a relative term, the absolute never attainable. But I
have been thinking lately what a zero of experience it is, comparatively, to have known the Franconia notch only as the tourist whom I have quoted. For in the last year I have passed
through it well nigh a score of times, at every season, and I
realize that I know it far better than before, just as you know
your friend only when you have seen his inmost soul in sternness and pleasantry, in expectation, and in disappointment. So,
assuming that my readers know best the notch of July and
August, the tourist's notch, come with me in other months,
afoot and awheel, in sleigh and on snowshoes, and see if you
will not enjoy it then.

In early October the temptation of the last trip of the White
Mountain express had taken me to Littleton by train, just at
the time of the most glorious autumn colors; a warm day, with
no suspicion of chill for the snow on Washington seemed to

belong to a different world. But on Monday morning how painfully thin was a summer outing suit against a wintry wind, clouded skies, and snow-squalls, as I started to wheel south. But my mind was on something higher as I passed through Franconia village,—on Bald mountain, the sentinel of the notch, on the clouds above Cannon and Garfield, on the snow and cloud which crowned Lafayette. The forests were dull under those skies, not bright as on Saturday and Sunday, but all to me was fascinating as ever, being in striking contrast to their appearance when I had last seen them, in the sunrise light of May 31…

…Cannon mountain is a mass of dull red and yellow deciduous trees, that dovetail into the dark spruce above, which in turns gives way to the new snow upon the perfect curve of the upper ledges, where the sun has nearly broken through. Echo lake, at our feet, is open, black, bordered with snow; one of the sternest color effects in nature. Then mighty Lafayette, his head among the clouds, his spurs, "like knotted muscles," not suggestive of finite strength, with the mystery that envelopes every cloud-wrapped peak. Squalls on the other mountains, no distant eastward view. Though chilled by the wind, we linger, fascinated by the wavering clouds. Just as we turn to go, Lafayette lifts his cap in courtesy; there is a glimpse of the rocky cone and summit, black and white; then down again comes the cap, this time over his ears, for, as we sweep past the Profile House, we face a driving snowstorm. Never have those walls of rock seemed so high and black, or the setting of the "Old Man" so fitting, as seen that day through the snow. Well might the house be closed, for who would care to stay there now, unless he loves to be alone with Nature's power?…

…It is only a little past eight o'clock, and the sun has not risen in the notch. I take on my camera at the Profile cottage and decline a ride on the bobsled with Mr. Davis, for I must stop to photograph the "Old Man." Profile lake is, of course, in the shadow, which reaches almost to the great face. On the mountain side, where in summer the foliage is so thick that the slope seems covered with soft drapery, the snow shows everywhere through the trees, and corresponding to the bare trunks, the Old Man's chin seems of sharper outline and his features more gaunt. The clouds fly past his face, and with numbing fingers I wait minute after minute for a clear sky. So against the blue I have him, the sunlight upon his face, the snow upon his forehead; the snow-white dome of the mountain behind, the shadowy woods and shadowed lake below...

...The last time I saw the notch, except as in imagination I have recalled it a thousand times, was when toward the last of May I once more wheeled through. I can linger a bit now to watch the birds. Though some who should certainly know thought differently, it seemed to many of us who lived in New Hampshire that the birds were uncommonly abundant in the spring of 1900. At any rate I well remember the wealth of feathers and of music that made that ride memorable. In the first place the piece of open at the foot of the hill, as one passes from Littleton to Franconia, is a real aviary, where it is my hope sometime to spend many an hour, for merely in passing a few times I have seen that it is alive with birds, but I have never been able to follow them up, though tantalized by unfamiliar songs. Then the woods and fields all along the road seemed full of them that day, and when I came to Franconia, to the house where I always call (for who could pass the man who led the way up the cone of Lafayette in the driving snow?), I exclaimed enthusiastically, "I would like to spend a week covering those fine miles!" But Mr. Torrey has told us of "May in Franconia," and I must hasten on...

...A "harricane" had visited the fine timber lands about Lonesome lake the fall before, and the forest was a wreck. But climbing in and out and up and over, I finally reach a prostrate trunk whence I can look across to the great Franconia range, and see the lake near me and the wooded domes to the north. The sky is overcast and it seems fitting. There are still traces of snow. My senses give no evidence of another human being in the world. But do I eat my lunch in silence? Not at all! My orchestra was the winter wren, and need any more be said to those who know him? Now in the distance, now close beside me, but still provokingly invisible, I hear this song, in perfect harmony with all else, the bird's interpretation of the woods and the mountains, in some way a real expression of what life among them means to him.

My last visit to the notch. Dear old mountains! I shall see you again, I trust, in summers to come, but never so familiarly as I have known you for the last few years. You have never treated me but kindly; under a sometimes cold exterior I have always found a warm heart. Happy the man who can enter your gates at will and catch the secrets of your life!

INDIAN LEGENDS

The Old Man of the Mountain
A Correspondent of the *Boston Transcript*

This legend appeared in the *Boston Transcript* in the mid-1860s. The original copy was found in an old scrapbook at the Dartmough College Library which unfortunately did not include the date or author of the article. The author must remain only: "A Correspondent of the *Boston Transcript.*" Reprinted courtesy of the Dartmouth College Library.

A CORRESPONDENT of the Boston *Transcript*, writing from the Profile House, gives the following pleasing legend of one of the most remarkable wonders of the mountain world:

Whoever visits the White Mountains of New Hampshire, does not soon forget that profile of the human face, carved in the solid stone, and known as the "Old Man of the Mountain."

Abruptly projecting from the receding side of the precipice, the profile stands out against the sky, fifteen hundred feet above the little lake below. There is no mistaking the features—the massive fore-head, the heavy brow; the sharply-defined nose;

the slightly-parted lips; the senile chin—all are there, chiselled by nature, complete, symmetrical, and with an expression of more than mortal sadness.

How came the profile there? By what cunning hand have been traced those lines of enduring sadness? Is the Old Man now what he ever has been, or was he once a living, sentient being? we asked, and in reply, as we gazed at his sad face from the shores of the little lake, received the following

LEGEND

Among these mountains there lived for ages undisturbed the Indian god Ulala. On the little plain near by stood his wigwam, facing the sun, which only at midday shone into this mountain fortress. A little beyond the plain, surrounded by towering walls of granite, its waters cool as an Alpine spring, there nestles a quiet lake. On its fair bosom he paddled his light canoe; from its sparkling depths, with a line of sinews he drew the frisky trout; along its pebbled shores he chased the timid deer, or sped his jasper-headed arrow swift to the very heart of the imprudent stag, which, in native vanity, sported with its mirrored self along the brink of its quiet waters; and ever when the shades of evening fell, he loved to commune with his departed braves, whose spirits as if conscious of the surrounding grandeur, still lingered on the misty mountain-tops, there to repeat again and again his every call.

For his people he exercised a paternal care. He told them where was found the evergreen hemlock from which their bows were made; he pointed out to them the hidden paths among the mountains; he taught them the medicinal properties of plants, how to bind up wounds, and by what magic to drive away evil spirits; he explained to them the mystery of their origin, the rites of religion, and the rewards which awaited only the brave in the land of the Hereafter.

Long and prosperous had been the reign of Ulala. Gaunt Famine had not entered the wigwams of his people. Consuming Fever was ever checked by his simple medicines, and his braves, strengthened by the life-giving air of the mountains, never failed in battle. Often did Ulala rejoice at his children's prosperity.—But an evil day brought from the south the pale man, scattering diseases in his path, and dealing death among Ulala's people. As he advanced, the red man retreated. Victory ever stayed with his terrible weapons. Ulala watched the unequal contest, and mourned over his vanquished and fleeing children. No longer was the song of the Indian maiden or the echoing whoop of the dusky warrior heard among these hills. Toward the setting sun the red men, torn and bleeding, turned their tottering foot-steps. Ulala climbed the mountain-side and watched with heavy heart and tearful eye their retreating forms. In the distance the athletic Indian became a speck—the speck, nothing—all was gone! A tear fell down the mountain-side and formed the little lake beneath. Suddenly his breath ceased— his forehead grew cold—his lips rigid, and the features of unhappy Ulala were transformed to this profile of enduring granite! And thus shall it ever remain, facing the eastern sky in grand but gloomy majesty; and as long as time shall endure, the traveller among these mountains will be reminded of the white man's cruelties, the red man's wrongs, as he gazes into the sad, stony features of Ulala, "The Old Man of the Mountain."

That Old Man and His Dream
Charles G. Chase

Privately printed in 1892, Charles Chase's *That Old Man and His Dream* is a legend that every modern reader would have wanted to witness. Chase's work was illustrated and printed by Livermore and Knight Co. of Providence, Rhode Island. Some of the unique illustrations are again reprinted here, but the identity of the artist, who signed his drawings "D.T.K.," is not known. Reprinted courtesy of the Dartmouth College Library.

I SUPPOSE NEARLY everyone who lives in this part of the world has either seen or heard of the "Old Man of the Mountain," in Franconia, New Hampshire. From the picture here given, those who have not seen him may form a very good idea of his appearance. What a stern looking old fellow he is, and how lone-some he must be, away up there on the mountain all alone!

His condition in winter must be fearfully desolate, for then the weather is icy cold, and few care to make him a visit. His friends at that season, prefer to be away under sunnier skies than those which then cover his mountain home.

I am told he very keenly feels this neglect and sometimes shows by a certain sarcastic look that he considers most of the friendships of this life largely dependent upon agreeable surroundings. Let a poor fellow once be left out in the cold, and how quickly many of his pretended friends will desert him. This the old man once muttered to himself on a cold winter night, when the stars were hid, and there was nothing about him but intense and awful solitude.

There are three very remarkable things about him, which thoughtful people must have observed. No one has ever been able to ascertain his age. Learned men have searched records

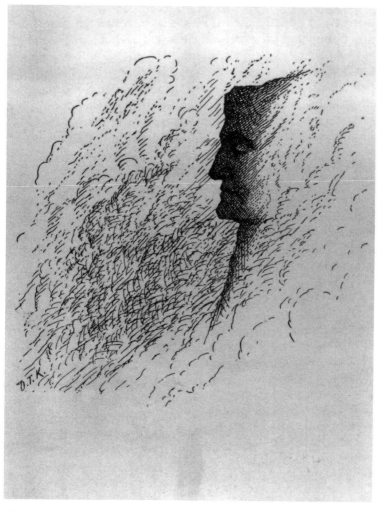

The Face of Stone. From *The Old Man and His Dream* by Charles
G. Chase. Illustrations by D.T.K. as reproduced in *The Franconia
Gateway* by G. Waldo Browne. From the author's collection.

THE GREAT STONE FACE

The Great Stone Face. From *The Old Man and His Dream* by Charles G. Chase. Illustrations by D.T.K. as reproduced in *The Franconia Gateway* by G. Waldo Browne. From the author's collection.

for it, but all their efforts to find out have been in vain. Then again, he never allows visitors to see but one side of his face. I saw him thirty years ago, and the same side was turned to me then, that is seen by visitors who go there now. Curious people have wondered why he is so particular about this, and some have gone so far as to suppose that he has warts, or ugly spots on the other side, which he wishes to hide. This may be true, and if it is, no one can blame him, for it is just the way other men would do, especially if they were liable, as he is, to be *kodaked* at any moment, by idle visitors. They certainly would hide their defects and try to appear faultless in the picture. Another peculiarity about him is, that he never allows any one to see him except at a distance. A great many people have climbed the mountain where he lives, for a nearer view than can be obtained from the valley below: but when they have come within a certain distance of him, he has always disappeared and left them only to guess where he had gone.

I have heard a great many stories about this old man, and, without vouching for their truth, I will relate one or two which I am sure will interest the reader.

It is said that years ago, an old Indian succeeded in getting into his presence. This was such a remarkable event, and so closely connected with one of the peculiarities of which I have spoken, I am sure all will agree that the particulars of it ought to be recorded. It occurred in this way: Years before, the Indian had made a visit to a tribe in the far south; (some have said it was to that one with which the brave and beautiful Indian girl was connected, who saved the life of Captain John Smith,) and while there, had become acquainted with the strange and remarkable weed which we now call tobacco. He had leaned how to smoke it, and not only that, but, with true Indian curiosity, had carefully noticed the effect produced upon those who used it. He saw that it had power to relax the muscles of a very stern face, and sometimes to produce warmth and geniality where only coldness and reserve were usually seen. Indeed, he had observed cases where people, when under its influence, sometimes told secrets which otherwise they might have had the good sense to keep to themselves. When he came home, he

WREATHS OF SMOKE

Wreaths of Smoke. From *The Old Man and His Dream* by Charles G. Chase. Illustrations by D.T.K. as reproduced in *The Franconia Gateway* by G. Waldo Browne. From the author's collection.

brought quite a quantity of this tobacco with him, and one day while smoking his pipe and looking upon the mountain, he conceived the idea of winning the good graces of the old man, by means of a pipe and tobacco. He said to himself, "If I can only once bring him under the influence of that magic weed, I shall not only be admitted to his presence, but allowed to talk with him on familiar terms, as friend with friend." How many conquests over other strong men have been made in this way, since then, I leave the reader to imagine. So he made a great pipe out of the root of a tree, and, taking that and some of his precious tobacco with him, he started up the mountain.

Fortunately, the wind that day, was blowing in the direction of the old man, and, when not very far off, the Indian blew from his own pipe, a full puff of smoke, directly into his face. The old fellow, instead of disappearing as the Indian feared he would do, kept his seat and appeared almost spellbound. Seeing this, the Indian felt sure the time had come for accomplishing his purpose, and summoning all his courage, he walked directly into the old man's presence, and offered him the pipe and tobacco which he had brought. Of course, those who never saw any signs of relenting in that stern and weather-beaten face will suppose the gift was indignantly refused. On the contrary, it was received with great eagerness, and after many expressions of gratitude and delight, and a few instructions imparted by the Indian, the old man sent out upon the clear atmosphere his first wreath of smoke.

Then began a long conversation between the two, in which the "Old Man of the Mountain" told the Indian many wonderful stories. I have made a great many inquiries, but could never find out exactly what the stories were. We can readily suppose what the character of them might have been. Perhaps they were about terrific storms which he had seen—storms that uprooted trees and hurled great rocks from the tops of the mountains to the valleys below; of times when the mountains were a great deal higher than they now are, and when their peaks were always covered with snow, and avalanches came thundering down their sides; of wild animals, many of which

OLD MAN OF THE MOUNTAINS SMOKING

Old Man of the Mountain. From *The Old Man and His Dream* by Charles G. Chase. Illustrations by D.T.K. as reproduced in *The Franconia Gateway* by G. Waldo Browne. From the author's collection.

are now extinct, that used to roam through the forests; of Indians who came to see him long before Lief Ericsson and his hardy Norsemen crossed the stormy Atlantic; of wonders which, from his sublime height, he had seen in the heavens above. Perhaps he said that in his youth he heard the grand anthem of the morning stars, spoken of in Sacred Writ. How I wish the old Indian had recorded the stories he told him, so that I might now publish them in a book.

The report is, that the interview lasted until nightfall, when the old man bade the Indian depart, and then, wrapping himself in a cloud, soon fell into a sound sleep.

That night he had a strange dream which filled him with anxiety and alarm. Like most dreams, it was much confused, but apparently was of serious import. It was about gatherings of excited men, rolls of lettered parchment, devastated forests, frightful explosions, raging fires lighting up the whole heavens, polluted streams of water, rumbling noises, snorting monsters darting through the valleys, hasty flights of birds, howlings of wild beasts; all so terrible, it is difficult to repeat the story without a shudder! Now the old man always attached great importance to dreams. He often had them, and would spend many of his waking hours in trying to make out their meaning. This special dream was so unusual and startling that for a while it absorbed all his thoughts. Indeed, it affected him so that for many nights he could not sleep. The only meaning which he could make out of it, was—that by-and-by, pale faced men would come into that region and make sad havoc of his old home: that in the name of what would be called a *State*, portions of his sublime inheritance would be seized and without sense, sentiment or shame, and only for a paltry sum, sold to selfish men who, to gratify a greed for gain, would cut down the grand old trees which for ages had adorned his mountain home; they would kill the wild animals that were his companions and pets; would frighten away the birds of beautiful plumage and song which always awakened him in the morning and cheered his early evening hours; they would defile the brooks and lakes where lived and disported the speckled trout; and in many ways shamefully deface the beauties and grandeur of his home. Now can the reader wonder that he was frightened when he awoke, and that he then made a vow which he has always faithfully kept—that no human being should ever again appear in his immediate presence.

I have heard another very singular story, which I think will be of interest to children.

An eagle once built her nest in the old man's nose. How she ever dared do it, I cannot imagine, for the danger was very great. If she had been found out, the old fellow, with one blast, would have sent her scooting down the side of the mountain. But I presume she did the work in the early morning, while he was asleep. "Now," said the eagle to herself, after the nest was done, "what a fine chance to hatch and bring up a family of eaglets! I am in a place sheltered from the storms, and where no one will think to hunt for my nest." So she laid her eggs and all went on very well, until the first eaglet was hatched, when she was so delighted to have become the mother of a little baby eagle, she began to flap her wings with all her might. This, of course, was a very imprudent thing to do, and she ought to have known better, for it tickled the old man's nose, so that he began to sneeze. Now, you know what a great commotion it makes when your mamma sneezes. Perhaps it bursts a few buttons from her dress, and frightens the kitty, which happens at the time to be sleeping before the fire; so you can understand what a sneeze from the old man must have been. It was so violent, all who heard it must have feared the "crack of doom" had finally come. Rocks and trees were sent flying through the air, bears and other wild animals, roaming in the forest, were frightened and scampered away, the eagle screamed, and some Indians who were fishing in a lake near by thought it thundered.

Now, my young friends, the next time you go to the White Mountains I wish you would find the oldest inhabitant of that region and ask him if these stories are probably true.

The Great White Hills
of New Hampshire

Ernest Poole

This third Indian legend appeared in Ernest's Poole's *The Great White Hills of New Hampshire* published in 1946. Poole, a native of Chicago, later owned a home in Franconia, New Hampshire. A graduate of Princeton University, he won the Pulitzer Prize in 1918. He died in January 1950.

WHEN IN the Glacial Age the ice had gouged that vast rift through our range, the sun through untold centuries shone down and clothed in green the bleak naked mountain pass. Pine forests grew and through them wandered deer and wildcat, bear and moose. Hunting them, the red men came and up at the head of the Notch they saw a great stone face frowning down from its cliff in the clouds. They worshiped him as a god and prayed to him to protect their homes from the Mohawks who raided from the west, and they left this legend of how he responded to their appeals.

When a band of Mohawk warriors had burned and massacred down below and been driven back by the Pennacooks, they returned up the long winding Notch trail and exhausted slept through the night. At sunrise they spied that great face frowning on them from the clouds. "It is the Manitou!" they cried. As they fell on their faces, darkness came, and out of thunder and lightning they heard the dreaded Manitou say:

"You have made war on your brothers and your hands are stained with blood! You have dared to enter this place of the Great Spirit unsummoned, and the penalty is death!"

As they lay trembling on the ground, lulled by a strange spellbinding song, they fell asleep and turned to stone and became the boulders found there still.

Franconia Notch, White Mountains, N. H. Postcard. The message on the postcard reads: "The Mountains are as beautiful as ever." From the author's collection. (Readers and visitors to Franconia Notch will recognize that this is a very liberal artistic impression of the notch and that it is not possible to have this view of the Old Man of the Mountain.)

Christus Judex,
A Traveller's Tale

Edward Roth

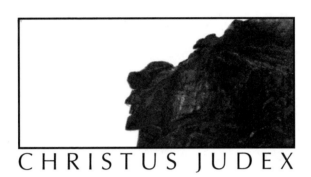

CHRISTUS JUDEX

Christus Judex, A Traveller's Tale
Edward Roth

Edward Roth's *Christus Judex* has been described as a "vivid romance" and by other authors as the "most beautiful story," the "most interesting story," and "the loveliest story" about the Profile.

In the history of the White Mountains, Roth, referred to as Professor Roth when he is infrequently mentioned, is known only for this single volume, first published in 1864 and today available only as a collector's item in rare-book shops. It has been reprinted in several editions, unabridged and abridged, including an 1892 edition printed by Charles H Greenleaf, the proprietor of The Profile House, in memory of his late partner at that hotel, Richard Taft.

Edward Roth was born in Kilkenny, Ireland, in 1826. It is not known when he moved to Philadelphia, but that is where he became an "educationalist." In 1863 he founded and became principal of the Broad Street Academy, a school for boys aged 6 to 18. The catalogs for that school show that he was also the author of many of the text books including those for: Latin, Arithmetic, Geography and Bookkeeping. Roth described the school and education as follows:

It has been the Principal's aim to establish in Philadelphia a home-school to receive pupils from the age of six to eighteen, where—the leading idea being to develop every good faculty, moral and physical, with which their Creator has endowed them—the range of instructions must be unusually wide, and nothing of importance omitted.

The use of tobacco being such a deleterious and widespread evil among growing boys, the Principal cannot receive into his school any pupil who does not honestly pledge himself to abstain from the drug, in any form, as long as he is a member of Broad Street Academy.

The undeniable advantage of a home-school over a boarding-school lies in securing to the parent the invaluable opportunity of always having the child under his own eye. Therefore, the Principal claims from the parent, as his right, as much earnest co-operation as possible in their joint task. The chief points in which he especially asks the parent's assistance are:

To have breakfast early enough for the child to be in school in time.

To have his clothing always neat, well-fitting and presentable.

To give him an opportunity every evening of preparing for school-work for at least one hour, and to see that he does it.

Roth continues:

... the day is passed forever when mere ability to read, write, and cipher can be called an education. You may do all that, and still be justly considered an ignorant man. Reading, writing, and ciphering can no longer dispel the clouds of ignorance, conceit, selfishness, rapacity, and dishonesty that are now rising, black and threatening, in every quarter of the sky. It is only *correct thought, real knowledge, just and broad observation, an undeviating sense of honor, and the heart and soul to stand by them all,* that the world now calls for more loudly than ever.

When and where Roth visited in the White Mountains is not known, and similarly, it will never be known what prompted Roth to write this story. However, from his other writings, it can be concluded that he had a very fertile mind. He authored a biography of Napoleon III that was published in 1856. In addition, he translated four of Jules Verne's books from the original French. Roth died in Philadelphia in 1911. In 1928 a former pupil described Roth as a man who "was preeminent as a scholar and an educator, and one who surrounded himself with a group of instructors well calculated to make worthy men of his pupils."

Readers may now again enjoy this White Mountain-Franconia Notch story written by the "educationalist" from Philadelphia.

Christus Judex, A Traveller's Tale

To his pupils, old and young, of
both hemispheres, the following
little story, suggested by the sight
of a well known wonder of nature,
is affectionately dedicated.
By E. R.
Philadelphia, 1864

CHAPTER I.

THE PICTURE

F ALL the villages which the tourist contemplates with
enraptured eye as he descends from the Alps into the
plains of Lombardy, Acqua Chiara is certainly not the
least beautiful. Its founder, however long ago he lived, must
have had a keen eye for the picturesque; for it is located on the
precise spot where it not only appears to the best advantage
itself, but also commands the most enchanting views afforded
by the Lago Dorno. The latter is one of those charming little
lakes so common in this country, which, as their basin lies between the sinking spurs of the distant Alps, are long, narrow,
and winding in shape, and disclose at every turn some new and
unexpected combination of light and shade, water and sky,
wood and rock, hamlet, chateau, island, hill, dale, and snowy
mountain. However, it is not my intention to describe the village or its beauties now, but to tell of an incident that befell me
there about fifteen years ago, which was of rather a singular
character.

The sun was just setting behind the Apennines as, weary
and footsore, I entered the village and directed my steps to the
first inn that presented itself. Neither the smiling *"Ben arrivato,
signor!"* of the bustling host, nor the substantial supper for

which I was indebted to my unmistakably outlandish air, nor the merry laughter of a group of young people dancing and singing under a large tree at the other side of the way, having succeeded in arousing me out of a kind of gloominess into which I sometimes cannot help falling, I retired early, in the hope of refreshing my exhausted energies with a good night's rest. In this I was altogether disappointed. I tossed and tumbled about for some hours, but could not fall asleep. At last I arose, dressed, and, tempted by the brilliancy of the moon and the coolness of the night, raised the window, and, my chamber being on the ground-floor, went out. After wandering about for some time, I found myself in front of the village church. The door was not locked; and, yielding to a habit my good grandmother taught me many years ago, I soon found myself saying a few prayers before the altar.

The moonlight streamed brightly in at the window, rendering everything around almost as visible as in the daytime. There was little interior ornament to be seen; but my attention was soon so completely engrossed by one object, that, to gaze at *it*, I disregarded everything else. Right over the altar was a large painting, containing one single figure. It did not represent the Crucifixion, as is generally the case with such pictures: on the contrary, the figure—of which I could distinctly see only the head—seemed to be sitting. But this head affected me most powerfully. It was the profile of a pale, noble countenance gazing sorrowfully yet immovably on some heart-rending sight. Oh, the sternness of that brow, though the eye was mild and the mouth gentle and loving! And the chin: it was the embodiment of inexorability: it told of strict justice, but no mercy. It might have passed for the face of Brutus superintending the preparations for the execution of his sons. Such a thought, indeed, at first occurred to me; but, of course, it was instantly rejected. Notwithstanding the relentlessness displayed in those features, there was something so surpassingly divine about the whole head, that the humblest peasant needed no informant to tell him that *that* was the beatified countenance of the Lord Christ.

But it was neither the beauty, nor the divine expression, nor the awful sternness, of the countenance that affected me now. In other circumstances, these wonders of art would have possessed their proper charm for my mind. But they were now completely disregarded in my feelings of the most profound astonishment. *The countenance was as familiar to me as my father's face, and yet I could not tell where I had seen it.* I had never been in the country before; in fact, it was only my second day in Italy. In vain I recalled to my mind the few faces I had thought deserving particular remark during my travels: not one possessed the most distant resemblance to that grand, impressive countenance gazing up there so sorrowfully yet with such awful sternness.

And yet, the longer I contemplated it the more intimately I found myself acquainted with every turn of the outline. That peculiarly shaped brow, straight and towering; that slightly aquiline nose, so suggestive of power and resolution; those lips, forcibly drawn in, as it were to repress or conceal their quivering; that chin, so square, so fixed, so feelingless;—all these I had often gazed on before, often studied with such interest that the very sight of them now forcibly recalled to my mind the various reveries into which I had often fallen whilst beholding them. Those features had sometimes filled my imagination with the idea of a mighty monarch slowly leading his disciplined legions against a tumultuous host of his subjects who had formerly regarded him with reverence and affection, but were now madly arrayed in arms against him, instigated by some fanatical watchward, At other times, every warlike expression would melt away, and the features became those of a genie, beneficent but submissive to command, who, being appointed by a higher power to superintend some direful punishment, would have willingly declined the task, but is now regretfully preparing for its strict and merciless execution. And at other times, I well recollected, they had seemed to bear the expression which the countenance of one of the giants of old might assume if he now looked out of his grave and saw all traces of his brethren's long sojourn on this earth swept away forever from its surface, and their places filled by a race, active indeed at present and full of life, yet destined, as he well knew, —themselves and their possessions,—to undergo a doom as sweeping, as complete, and as utterly inevitable as that which had befallen their now forgotten predecessors.

These and similar thoughts arising in my mind at the present moment, almost immediately at the sight of this picture, convinced me beyond all doubt that I had seen the face before. Something seen in a dream could not have left such vivid impressions, and no face with which I had not been at least for some time closely acquainted could have excited such a continuous chain of ideas. My father's humble cottage in distant America had contained no picture capable of attracting my attention or exciting my youthful imagination so powerfully; and the splendid masterpieces of the Continent I had merely glanced at, or omitted to notice altogether, reserving for some future occasion a critical examination of their charms. None of my relations or intimate friends, none of the great men either of my own country or the few whom I had contrived to see in Europe, bore these features.

Whose were they, then? This question I asked in vain. I felt as if in a dream; and the cool night-air that swept over me as I left the church hardly restored me.

Late as it was, the landlord stood at the door on my return.

"I have been to your chapel," said I.

"The signor is fond of praying by moonlight."

"I might have prayed, but—"

"The signor is pale: has he seen a ghost?"

"Not exactly: something nearly as bad."

"Ah! some furious brigand—"

"No: nothing of the kind. Who painted the picture over the altar of your church?"

"The signor has seen our picture?"

"I wish to know who painted that picture, and whom it represents."

"The signor takes uncommon interest in our picture."

"With good reason. I am intimately acquainted with the

person that bore those features."

"Basta! The signor has a good memory."

"How long has that picture been there?"

"Exactly one hundred and fifty years come to-morrow."

"One hundred and fifty years! Impossible! The picture over the altar? It is quite new."

"There is but one picture in the church, and that is over the altar,—*Il Cristo Giudicante* ('The Judging Christ'). This day one hundred and fifty years ago it was hung up in the church, and tomorrow we celebrate its one hundred and fiftieth anniversary. We are proud of that picture, signor. It was a native of Acqua Chiara that painted it. He is our only great artist, it is true; but he is a *great* one. You can see his tomb tomorrow covered with flowers."

How much farther the voluble *Locandiere*—who evidently took me for a Protestant— may have gone on, I do not now remember; for his extraordinary assertion regarding the hundred and fifty years completely bewildered me. Here was mystery upon mystery. At first, the greatest and most puzzling difficulty is to decide to which of my acquaintances these features belong; but now it appears that they are those of a being not only not in existence at present, but who lived one hundred and fifty years ago. I must be mistaken. I have perhaps been led astray by some imperfect resemblance, and my heated imagination easily supplied what else was wanting. In the present state of my feelings this is not at all unlikely; and to-morrow I shall probably laugh heartily at my perplexity. Thus I tried to reason with myself for a moment; but the least reflection again showed the improbability of this supposition. The impression made on my mind by these features originally had been too distinct, too deep, to admit the possibility of a mistake now. The moment I saw them, I had recognized them; and, what was more, they had called up the very same train of ideas (from their familiarity I must have been entertaining them for a long time) as I had often fallen into formerly when contemplating the original, somewhere or other, at my leisure. Feverish and restless, I lay awake all that short summer-night, harassing myself in a fruitless attempt to solve these irreconcilable difficulties; and it was not until morning had dawned that I could at last obtain a few hours of undisturbed repose.

CHAPTER II.

THE CHURCHYARD.

THE cheerful sounds of the Sunday-morning bell soon dispelled my slumbers; and, upon going out of the inn, I found the little village in an unusual state of excitement. The men, young and old, dressed in their tastiest holiday attire, were hastening through the street, their faces bright and beaming, and their looks not without an air of importance. The women, too, evidently took great interest in the *fete*. The Italian maiden, ever graceful in form and spiritual in expression, never looks so well as on Sunday. That sacred day always seems to shed something of its own soothing and sanctifying influence on her, which is inexpressibly charming. On this morning, however, the brilliancy of the new dresses, the profusion of ribbons, flowers, bouquets, and silver pins, and the increased animation so generally perceptible among the female inhabitants of Acqua Chiara, lent them such additional lustre, that I was not at all surprised that many young men found unusual difficulty in getting past certain doors and windows underneath which their path lay.

The cause of all this pleasing bustle soon appeared. On my arrival at the church, I found the entrance all decorated with flowers, and the surrounding graveyard crowded with people, who were decking the graves, old and new, with garlands and roses. To the right, about half-way between the church and the farthest bounds of the graveyard, through the moving crowd, I could distinguish a large, white monument. Upon approaching nearer, I found it was erected in the middle of about two rods square of greensward, which was enclosed within an elegant iron railing. It consisted of two marble pillars, about eight feet high, supporting an arch, and enclosing a bust, underneath which was cut, on a slab, in large, conspicuous letters,—

PIETRO CASOLA
PAINTER OF THE JUDGING CHRIST
NATIVE OF ACQUA CHIARA.
BORN 1655. DIED 1725.
REQUIESCAT IN PACE.

Although, as I was assured by a bystander, the monument was nearly one hundred years old, it looked as if it were erected yesterday; and now, decorated as it was with roses and flowers and wreaths twisted around the pillars, it really presented a very interesting spectacle.

In answer to my further inquiries, my informant brought to my mind a great deal of what Battista Pientone, my worthy host, had already told me the preceding night, but to which I had paid little attention, from the confusion into which the first part of his intelligence had thrown me. After learning now that it was one of the most inviolable customs of the inhabitants of Acqua Chiara to celebrate every tenth year the installation of the picture, with all the splendor and *eclat* that their humble means afforded,—

"Is '*Il Cristo Giudicante*' his only work?" I asked.

"Signor, yes: his only *great* work. But a few small pieces of his are still in the possession of the neighbors, and a few, I understand, are to be found in the great palace at Florence."

"It is certainly an extraordinary piece of art," said I, earnestly.

"*E mirabilissimo, signor!*" cried my informant, delighted at my fervor.

"But don't you think it looks very fresh?"

"It does look fresh; but I have been for more than fifty years gazing at it, Sunday after Sunday, not to mention the week-days, when I was troubled in heart from one thing or another, and would come in to look at it and get consolation. For that face is so stern-looking, signor, that a sight of it, reminding us of what we all have to expect, forces us to disregard trifling annoyances. Oh, signor, it is impossible to tell how many quarrels that picture has prevented in our village, and how much good it has done generally. People coming here, as they do sometimes, from Monti, Chiusa, and even from Milan, have often declared that the sight of that head succeeded in recalling them to a proper sense of their duties to God and man, when every other means had failed. But, as I was saying, I have looked on that face every Sunday for the last fifty years, and often and often besides, and I can assure you that it appears now precisely the same in all respects as when I saw it for the first time. The old men of our village declare that it looked no brighter the first day it was hung up than it does now, and that it seemed as if the love and regard the people here entertain for it keeps it always fresh and bright. Indeed, there is a kind of prophecy among us that denounces terrible woes on the village as soon as that picture begins to look dim; and, though there is no regular authority for this prophecy, for my part I cannot altogether disbelieve it."

"Is it known whose face it represents?"

"Whose face? Whose but the Lord Christ's?"

"You are aware, of course, that all painters have *models*, and—"

"Oh, I understand the signor now. But though this picture was painted here, no native of this village ever sat for it; indeed, no mortal being ever sat for it. Casola himself often declared that no man ever lived in this world that bore those features."

"Those features never had a real existence?"

"So he often declared. He was absent in a distant country for a long time. On his return—but it is too long a story to tell now; and here comes the Padre, who knows it best: he will, no doubt, be pleased to relate it all to you at the first opportunity."

My renewed astonishment was here interrupted by the arrival of the procession. It was headed by the Padre, dressed in his usual garments; and the little boys and girls that followed him, two by two, instead of candles bore wreaths and flowers in their hands. He stopped at the entrance of the little enclosure, and the children, filing off, one by one, the girls to the right, the boys to the left, outside the railing, continued their march until they met on the opposite side, when the whole line stopped, and remained standing at the distance of about a foot from the railing, which they exactly enclosed.

Then came the old men and matrons of the village,—venerable beings, who perhaps for the last seventy or eighty years had not missed a single one of these joyous commemorations. They also filed off right and left, taking their places behind the children. After these came the young unmarried men, to the number of one hundred, bearing wands waving with ribbons, and wearing pretty breastknots in front of the left shoulder. They filed to the right and left like the others; but, before they had all passed, the sound of voices in chorus was heard, and presently twelve young men dressed as artists—natives, as I was informed, of the nearest parts of Northern Italy, and at present either painters or painters' pupils—proceeded slowly by, chanting a song which some poet had made long ago in honor of the great Casola.

After the artists, at some distance, came a triumphal car, borne on the shoulders of twelve of the youngest married men. In this chair, under a canopy that represented the starry sky, holding a cross in her hand, was seated a young maiden about twelve years of age, beautiful as a star, and dressed in the purest white. She represented Religion, and was without ornament of any kind except her own radiant beauty. Two young maidens, emblematic of Poetry and Painting, went before her, strewing the path with flowers. Then followed the unmarried village maidens, clad in gay costumes of various colors, crowned with flowers, and singing another song which a poetess had composed in praise of the great painter. Last of all came another maiden, arrayed in white, only a long black veil of the finest texture, falling from her head, floated gracefully over her shoulders almost down to the ground. Personating the gratitude of the inhabitants of Acqua Chiara, she was the most beautiful girl that could be found; and now she bore a large emblematic garland, to the composition of which every family in the village had contributed its share.

As soon as the leaders of the artists had reached the rails, all separated and halted, forming a line on each side of the path, through which the supporters of the chair, and afterwards the maidens, passed. I should have mentioned that, at the commencement of the ceremony, the Padre, near whom I had chanced to be, seeing that I was a stranger, had courteously beckoned me to his side, so that I had every opportunity of enjoying the scene.

As soon as the triumphal car reached the monument, the supporters turned to the right and let down their burden. In the mean time the maidens still advanced; but they ceased singing as they entered the enclosure, which they nearly filled. It was a moment of universal silence and breathless interest when the veiled maiden approached the monument, knelt before it, and kissed the white marble. Then, with one accord, burst from the lips of the assembled multitude the song always sung on such occasions.

It was a simple air, and the words were artless, not to say unpolished; but it is impossible to describe the effect produced on me by the harmony, heightened as it was by the sight of the numberless faces beaming with love, joy, and gratitude, and many streaming with tears in the enthusiasm of the moment. To translate the *spirit* of the song is beyond my power: the following, though a feeble, is a pretty literal translation of the words:—

SONG

O loved Casola. painter great and good,
    Once more before thy treasured shrine we meet
Again the memory of that day's renew'd
    When first thy fellow-men thy work did greet,—
When, first display'd before their spell-bound eyes,
    Its meaning struck them with mysterious dread,
And made them, trembling, almost realize
    The awful judgment that awaits the dead.
Its meanings *still* remain in all their force;
    Thy gift, O Christian, *still* its office fills;

Still is it found a never-failing source
    Of sweet relief for all our human ills;
The very worst we suffer here is naught,
    If yet our hearts from sin continue pure:
Ah, who can dare indulge one sinful thought,
    And then a glance from that stern face endure?
Then, loved Casola, here, upon thy grave,
    Thy happy people meet in gratitude
To bless and praise the glorious God that gave
    Our feeble wills a help so great and good.
And may He grant that thy example bright
    Our youth may imitate! and, oh, may He
Preserve thy *work*,—our glory, our delight,—
    To bless our latest coming sons in *thee!*

When the strains had died away, the kneeling maiden rose, and amid another universal hush of silence, advanced to the bust, kissed the lips, and carefully laid the garland on the brow. This, perhaps, was the moment of the most intense interest on the part of these good people. The old men and young women, I remarked, seemed most affected. The faces of the young men, it struck me, betokened rather pride and joy. Suddenly the bell, bursting into loud peals, summoned us to the church. The veiled maiden withdrew to her chair, where she remained whilst the procession retired slowly and silently, reversing the order of the approach. As the children returned, they met, two and two, before the tomb, and deposited their wreaths on the space before the grave, and, when that was covered, they hung them in festoons on the railing that surrounded the enclosure.

CHAPTER III.

THE CHURCH.

N my entrance into the church, my eyes first naturally sought the "Cristo;" and, now that I could see it more plainly in the daylight, it occurred to me that, while the features appeared exactly as they had the previous night, the expression had become more benign. Of the hard, stony sternness that was so terrifying at first, though it had not entirely vanished, I could hardly now catch a trace. This I imputed to the effect of the blaze of hundreds of tapers that surrounded the altar, softened and mellowed by the many-colored rays of the bright sun streaming in through the old windows of richly-stained glass. But I was afterwards told that the people also noticed this change, and that it had been often before remarked on such a day.

Clouds of incense now began to rise. The organ pealed forth the *Kyrie Eleison*, and mass commenced. I too must have partaken of the general enthusiasm and piety; for on no other occasion, however solemn, before or since, have I felt so deeply moved while present at the holy sacrifice. I was kneeling exactly opposite the picture, and, as I gazed on it, I felt myself gradually forgetting my familiarity with the features, and slowly imbibing a feeling far more absorbing and profound. As it was surrounded with wax lights, the frame was hidden in the blaze, the background faded away into distance, and the figure seemed to come out so distinctly that it required little imagination to believe it sat there living and breathing. All seemed to share in this impression; for, when the organ ceased, the stillness of death prevailed through the church, though every lip moved in prayer.

Mass went on. The Gloria was chanted, and the Credo. After the obligation, all was again hushed in the most profound silence.

Just then, a low, faint sound was heard from the organ. A silvery voice of surpassing sweetness chimed in, and, as the united sounds gradually rose, they were joined by the other voices of the choir, rolling forth rich volumes of delicious harmony. The words, which could be plainly distinguished, were those of a Latin hymn, which was neither rhyming nor metrical, but, like the Te Deum, consisting of detached sentences. The music was thus more expressive. Unbound by the regular rises and cadences, it rose or fell, sunk or swelled, according to the meaning of the sentiment. It was in complete harmony with all that I had witnessed in that strange church; for, though of a profoundly melancholy character, it contained occasional passages so beautiful and touching that one could easily suppose them to be uttered by a chorus of angels, as, rapt in awe, they witnessed the accomplishment of one of the tremendous mysteries of the *Eternal*. The words were simple, and to the following effect:—

HYMN

Before the world was made, and the stars, was the Lord
    Christ;
Rejoicing in the bosom of His Eternal Father;
And their Divine Love filled limitless space.
And countless ages rolled away.
At last Man was created, but by sin he disobeyed his
    Creator.
And because Man had offended against Omnipotent
    Justice, it grieved the Lord Christ.
For the Lord Christ loved Man as the apple of his eye.
And the Lord Christ became Man, and died to save us
    from Omnipotent Justice.
And He opened us the road to our home in Heaven.
And He still assists us on the way thither.
For the mercy of the Lord Christ is inconceivably great.
And He shall continue to assist us as long as the world
    endures.
But woe to the man that forgets the love of the Lord
    Christ,
Or disregards His guidance, or despises His admonitions.
On the Last Day shall all be made manifest.
Then shall Mercy be suspended, and Justice alone shall
    prevail.
Then shall His countenance be like a stone.
Against the terrors of that dreadful day enable thy servants
    to provide, O pious Lord!
Grant us the grace to imitate Thy example,

And to follow Thy guidance, and to practise Thy admoni-
tions,
That we may dwell with Thee for eternity;
For we are the children of Thy Father.

Towards the middle of the hymn, the music—of which an
indescribable grandeur and solemnity had been the chief char-
acteristic—gradually became strongly expressive of terror. It
impressed the listener, in spite of himself, with a sense of mortal awe and undefined fear. He felt an icy thrill in his heart, as
if in presence of a spirit. Upon me this feeling grew stronger
and stronger, until the choir came to the words, "*His countenance shall be like a stone,*" when a flash of terror shot through
me; for a glance at the "Cristo" now showed the countenance
transfigured indeed and divine, but hard and pitiless as a flinty
rock. This idea, of course, could only be attributed to the excited state of my feelings; but the writer and the composer of
the hymn had fully understood the conception of the painter.

But I will not detail much further my recollections of the
proceedings of that mass, however interesting they may be to
me, or deeply impressed as they are on my memory. I will not
dwell on the points of the moving discourse the Padre pronounced on the occasion, or on his joy at recognizing the countenances of many who had been present at the previous
celebration, or his touching allusions to the absence of others,
then so conspicuous, but *now* passed away forever, or his hearty
welcome to the strangers that honored their festivity, or his
warm earnestness when depicting the indebtedness of the village to their great painter, or his passionate admonitions to the
young artists then present to turn their glorious gifts to good
account, like Casola, to promote the happiness and virtue of
their brethren, and not to imitate too many others who make
their heaven-born art a slave to their vanity, if not an instrument for their destruction. "For *that* is real glory," cried the
good priest,—" *that* is genuine fame. *That* is why we love and
bless our own Casola. He is still among us: he is not dead. *His*
great heart has indeed ceased to beat; but through his great

work he still makes *ours* throb in our bosoms. His tongue is silent; but through his great work he is still as eloquent as Solomon. His arm has become ashes; but through his work he still takes the poor man consolingly by the hand and guides him to that bright home where poverty and suffering have an end. Through his work he is, and has been for one hundred and fifty years, loving us, protecting us, instructing us, and consoling us. And here his labors do not end. He will do the same for our descendants: they too will find him a benefactor. And let us confidently trust that in the future times, when all recollection of *our* short existence shall have vanished from the earth, when our children's children, to the fifth generation, shall have passed away, that even then the inhabitants of Acqua Chiara shall honor his memory, celebrate his festival, and bless his name as sincerely, as fervently, and as enthusiastically as we do now."

Mass proceeded and ended. Never before had I even imagined the existence of such pious enthusiasm as I had witnessed on that day. Never before had the paramount object of man's existence in this world been so powerfully brought home to my conviction. And yet the first feelings of surprise with which I had regarded the picture remained as vivid as ever. The question I asked myself oftenest on my departure from the church was, "Where *had* I seen that face?" The long and careful examination I had given it in the full light of day had only further convinced me, if that were possible, that I had often and often gazed on it before. Yet it was painted by a man who lived one hundred and fifty years ago. Nay, had I not been told that the features were not those of a human being at all? And this last assertion, though, of course, too evidently the offspring of ignorance or of extraordinary exaggeration to be believed, was still quite bewildering in its tendency. In a word, I was as much mystified as ever; but I was resolved to make every effort to solve the problem before leaving Acqua Chiara.

Returning to the inn, I was overtaken by a boy, who said that the Padre would be pleased to see me at his house. The invitation, as may be supposed, was readily accepted. Nothing could exceed the cordiality of my reception by the good Padre.

"At first sight," said he, "I knew you were an American; but the respectful interest you took in our little proceedings convinced me you were also a Christian." (Only Catholics are called Christians in Italy.)

"All your proceedings, sir," I replied, "possessed much attraction for me. The emotion of the people was quite affecting."

"Yes: the poor people love Casola sincerely. I never have to stir them up on *that* point. On the contrary, I fear," he added, smiling, "they sometimes think him quite as good a saint as any that has his name on the calendar."

"That is not surprising, Father: it is a magnificent picture. But that countenance, Father,—where did Casola see the original? or is it a creation of his fancy?"

"It is no creation of his fancy."

"It *is* the face of a man, then. Who was he? Where did he live?"

"No man that ever lived bore that countenance."

"It was not painted from a human countenance! It is not a creation of his imagination! Yet it is an original painting! You speak in riddles, Father."

"Yet in perfect truth, my son."

"Listen, Father. Yesterday, for the first time in my life, I set foot in your village; yet I have often seen that countenance before."

"Even that is not impossible; though you are the first man I ever heard make such an assertion."

"I see," he rejoined, as I was ready to break forth into a torrent of questions,— "I see that it is no ordinary curiosity you entertain about the matter; but I have no time to satisfy it now, as I have still many things to attend to. I will be happy to explain every thing to your satisfaction this evening, if you will honor my table with your presence. Casola's story is rather singular; but I have been hearing it from my childhood, and I know the most remarkable incidents of his life. Besides, a friend of the great artist, to whom he had bequeathed his papers, wrote a ' Life of Casola,' with a view towards publication, which, for some reason, never was published. This manuscript I have in my possession; and I think you will find it quite satisfactory on many points. I have never been in your great country; but what I have seen in this manuscript makes me regard it with redoubled interest. Excuse me now: I must attend to Vespers. *Addio!*"

From the particulars which the Padre so courteously imparted that evening, as well as from the full and circumstantial account which I myself read out of the manuscript, I contrived, on my return to the inn, whilst the chief details were still fresh in my memory, to write out the following history of Casola.

CHAPTER IV.

CASOLA'S APPRENTICESHIP.

 IOVANNI CASOLA possessed an independent fortune in Acqua Chiara, where his well known prudence and kindness of disposition had gained him universal good will. He was approaching his fortieth year when he married Beatrice Caracci. She was a native of Bologna, and a member of that wonderful family that had given to the world so many great painters. Pietro was their only child. From his earliest years he had given decided proofs of his talents for painting, and several portraits of his friends are still preserved which he took before he reached his twelfth year. His mother, who had much of the genius belonging to her family, was delighted at these efforts, and encouraged him to persevere in his course. Her greatest wish was to see him an artist; but, as she was a woman of exceeding piety and benevolence, she wished him to devote his talents to religious subjects only. "How noble," she sometimes exclaimed, in her conversations with her son, "how divine, is the inspired artist's calling when he renders back to Heaven the Heaven-bestowed gift! What magic influence he exercises over the souls of his fellow-beings! Who can view Raphael's Transfiguration without being thrilled with al-

most the same awful happiness as the real visible presence of the Redeemer would inspire? Contemplate the entranced countenance of Guido's Madonna in Florence, and you will soon commence to pray. Many have felt their angry passions soothed down and their souls filled with calm resignation at the sight of the sweet figures of Carlo Dolce. Even before the St. Mark of Fra Bartolomeo, as in the presence of a superior being, it is impossible to stand without feeling one's self filled with grand and ennobling thoughts. Oh, my son, fame has great charms for mortals; but, if thou hast genius, let it be thy aim rather to inspire men with just reflections regarding *their own condition* than with admiration for *thy great works*. After death, the breath of man, expended in censure or approbation, will be of little consequence to thee; but even the angels cannot enjoy a greater delight than their consciousness of having helped one poor soul on its way home to the bosom of its Creator. Pietro, the day I saw you paint a worthy picture, I would feel that the worldly object of my existence was accomplished. I would bless God and die."

"Mother," exclaimed Pietro, one day, after hearing her utter such sentiments with more than usual warmth,—"mother, what picture shall I paint? How can I benefit men?"

"Keep them in mind of the end of this life: that is as much as mortal may attempt. Paint Christ coming to judge the world."

"*Rex tremendae majestatis!*" cried the boy, as in ecstasy. "I will do it. Let *that* be the great object of my life. From this moment, to the accomplishment of that task I devote every faculty of my soul. Mother, let me begin!"

Through his mother's influence he was sent to Bologna. The most famous school in all Italy was held there at that time by Cignani. Casola, naturally of a highly spiritual temperament, and now entirely full of his noble project, surrendered himself with intense delight to the study of all those splendid creations of art by which he was surrounded. His master's talents were so highly esteemed that he had been ennobled by the title of Count; but his commissions for the execution of pictures had been so numerous as to prevent him from taking the steps necessary to attain the highest degrees of excellence; otherwise it was thought he would have rivalled Correggio or even Raphael. Casola became his favorite pupil; and, when Cignani removed to Forli, to paint the cupola of the church of the Madonna del Fuoco, he accompanied him, and occasionally wrought under his eye, for several years, at that great work.

During this time, the promise he had made his mother was ever uppermost in his mind. Enthusiastically bent on its successful accomplishment, he devoted every moment to the study of the principles of art as he could trace them in the works of the great masters. His opportunities were abundant. From the works of his venerable master alone he obtained deep glimpses into the mysteries of art. In the Farnese hall of the Palace in Bologna, where Cignani had executed his famous historical frescoes, the young painter found enough for a long time to satisfy his craving after the beautiful and the grand. But Bologna, besides being one of the oldest cities in Italy, was one of the most renowned for the cultivation of the arts. It contained pictures more than five hundred years old. Many of the most famous productions of the Italian mind, both in painting and sculpture, were collected there. The Venetian, Florentine, and Roman schools were fully represented, and the great Bolognese masters—from Guido da Bologna down to Domenichino—had enriched it with their grandest efforts. It was, however, to the works of Titian, Guido, Correggio, and more especially to those of the Caracci, that Casola particularly devoted his attention.

In the midst of all these treasures, his creative power was soon developed. When he was only fourteen years of age, he painted into a picture of his master's, that represented the Infant Christ among his companions, the figure of a child so beautiful and angelic, that Cignani, upon seeing it, burst into tears of admiration, and at once saluted him as one destined to become a master of Italian art. On another occasion he painted a small Œdipus Coloneus, in which the desolation of the old king was so forcibly expressed, and the style of the antique so rigidly imitated, that many found difficulty in believing it not to be a genuine Grecian relic. Still he pursued his studies, patiently, hopefully, and devotedly, until he had reached his twenty-third year, when, regarding his preparatory course as nearly finished, he began to think it was time to make a commencement of his promised work.

CHAPTER V.

FAILURE.

THE MANY attempts which he had heretofore made in that respect had been extremely unsatisfactory. His mind, though naturally of a serious and rather gloomy cast, found little difficulty in producing pleasant, even mirthful, images; and forms of grace and beauty grew almost spontaneously beneath his pencil. But the grand, the solemn, the sublime, had ever eluded his most vigorous searchings. In vain did he study and restudy the most precious specimens of the antique. Ancient art, he felt, contained nothing that approached the embodiment of a Christian's idea of a God of *Justice*. He left the antiques, and studied human countenances exclusively, but with no better success. Among them all he could find no model to assist him in portraying the tremendous idea that had taken possession of his soul, but which he was conscious he could never represent without such aid.

He went to Florence; but all the splendors of ancient and modern art collected in that famous city, though they served to exalt still higher his conceptions of ideal grandeur, did not furnish him with the assistance he required. He went to Rome, to visit, among other objects, Michael Angelo's wonderful work in the Sistine chapel, which he had often heard described in terms of rapturous admiration. But even the *"Last Judgment"*— the grandest effort in painting ever accomplished by man— did not satisfy him. He felt that the countenance of the

Omnipotent Judge, as represented there, did not realize *his* idea of the terrific grandeur which shall emanate from the face of the *Divine* REDRESSER on the awful day when his Justice is to be made manifest to all men.* Successive journeys to Naples, Venice, Mantua, Genoa, and Sienna, did not advance him nearer to the object of his desires. Remembering that Leonardo da Vinci, when painting his "Last Supper," had been for a long time in the same difficulty as himself, not being able to find an ideal for his Christ, he went to Milan, and visited the Refectory of the Dominicians of Santa Maria delle Grazie, where the picture was to be seen, to try how far he had succeeded at last. He was awestruck at the sublime calmness and conscious omnipotence displayed in the Saviour's countenance; but, of course, it was altogether devoid of that terror-inspiring expression that should belong to the avenging Judge.* His sharp eye also easily discovered that the head was left unfinished, as if the great master had given up the task in despair. Greatly discouraged, but still fully resolved to persevere, Casola was hesitating as to his next step, when a letter from his mother, announcing his father's rather sudden death, brought him back to Acqua Chiara. He found his mother in deep distress; but he exerted himself like an affectionate son, to calm her sorrow and console her for her loss.

Some weeks after they had discharged their melancholy duties towards the departed beloved one, and when the keenest pangs of grief were over, their conversation one day turned on the subject of the picture. Casola related all his difficulties, and again repeated an account of the means he had taken to overcome them. He had thoroughly studied the most magnificent of the ancient statues and basso-relievos, the grandest works of the modern great masters, and the most appropriate

---

* In the manuscript were many criticisms on the merits of the various collections of sculpture and painting seen by Casola in his travels, which I have not deemed it necessary to transcribe.

* It is perhaps needless to inform the reader that at the time of Casola's visit the "Last Supper" was still in a good state of preservation.

living models that he could find; yet, after all, he had not met anything to assist him to present in visible form the idea of the Judging Christ, which still lay clear and distinct in his own mind. After he had done speaking, he observed that his mother continued to look at him for some time in silence and with a thoughtful air, as if reflecting more on what his words had suggested than on what they had actually conveyed. At last she exclaimed, fervently, "Glory to the Divine Goodness! Even the most trifling act done in its holy name it never allows to pass unnoticed. It is not a year since I was told that a stranger, a priest, on his way to Rome, had been suddenly taken ill at the inn here, and that little hopes were entertained of his recovery. I went to see him immediately, and found him quite insensible and almost dead. He was a very old man, and his constitution, which evidently had been once of extraordinary vigor, was now completely broken. The physician said that with proper treatment and some stimulants he might yet be restored to consciousness and some strength, but he despaired of prolonging his life. In consequence of our incessant attention, in effect, he was able to converse in a few days, and then we learned that he was a French Jesuit, named De Seranne, who had spent the greater part of his life in the wildernesses of America. Upon his recall a few months previous, he had returned to Europe, and had been the bearer of important documents, some of which had caused great excitement in Paris as soon as their contents were known. They told of the discovery of that mighty river upon whose banks the French king intends to found a great Western empire. He had also brought letters to different parts of Germany and Switzerland; and it was to the effects of a terrible snow-storm which he had encountered when leaving the latter country that he ascribed his late sudden attack. He wrote a letter to Rome, but he was dead before the arrival of his friends. He preserved his senses to the last moment, and on the morning before his death he conversed with me calmly and cheerfully. I spoke about you and the great object you had in view in cultivating your profession so earnestly. When I spoke of the subject of your picture, he became quite animated. 'Ah!'

he exclaimed, 'I often wished that I only were a painter. I have seen the countenance such as might belong to a Judging Christ. In the dark wildernesses of America is a face which one cannot look at without shuddering,—tranquil, majestic, divine, but terrible! Let your son look on *that* face, and then paint a Judging Christ.' I thought his expression singular; but I did not deem it prudent just them to question him any further. They seemed prompted by the sudden recollection of some exciting incidents of his life among the savages, and the recital might exhaust his remaining strength."

"Did he say no more?" cried Casola, who had listened with breathless interest to his mother's narration.

"Only a few words expressive of his emotions when he heard an account of the mysterious face from the Indians for the first time."

"But what was its nature?"

"That he did not state. He saw it in the deserts of America; and, as far as I could understand, I think it is there still."

"That is enough. Mother, my resolution is taken. I will start for America."

"Pietro, I cannot oppose you. I see the finger of Providence in it all. I may not see you again for many years; but I feel convinced that I shall see you and your picture before I die. My desire to see it, and my conscious conviction that I shall see it, will keep me alive until your return. Go, my son; and, when you are among the deserts and waters of that wild world, remember that a mother's lips are imploring God for your protection and the accomplishment of your pious enterprise!"

"Mother, I feel like a new man. I share your confidence in my success. I am not to die in America. My bones are to rest beside yours, mother, in our own churchyard, where my father sleeps."

Casola departed with the intention of returning in five years, if alive, although on that point he seems to have entertained few apprehensions. He did not go directly to America, but first visited Spain, where he saw Murillo, in the midst of his great works in Seville. His journal of these travels, in many places copied fully and literally into the manuscript, was full of details regarding this visit, which, however, are not necessary to be given here. Many of the portraits which Murillo painted, of the proud nobles and melancholy beauties of the Spanish nation, Casola greatly admired. He considered them to have fully embodied the chivalrous yet grave spirit of a land teeming with the grandest legends of romance, and full of the most glorious as well as the most mournful records of history.

He visited Paris, where Le Brun, then at the height of his popularity and enjoying the most flattering attentions of his sovereign, was generally regarded as the great monarch of art in France. His pictures, illustrating the life of Alexander the Great, Casola considered full of genius; but the work at which he was then engaged—a series of paintings for the gallery at Versailles, representing the exploits of Louis the Fourteenth—in his opinion were not likely to answer the public expectations.

CHAPTER VI.

THE NEW WORLD.

AT LAST, on the 2d of May, 1680, he embarked at Rochelle for the New World. His voyage was very favorable; and, before the month was ended, his companions on board the "La Fleur," though they still could see nothing but a boundless waste of waters, were told that they were in the mouth of the St. Lawrence. As they proceeded up that noble stream, the low and desolate coast became gradually more visible. Flat, sandy hills and monotonous eminences bounded the view for a long time. No grass or shrubs could be seen. Like a man of great abilities to do good, which he does not choose to exert, so, Casola thought, the St. Lawrence here flowed sullenly and silently through a dreary desert, without affording it the means to nourish a single tree, but, in return, without receiving from its bosom a single tributary stream. Another day's sail, however, completely changed the scene, and henceforward the voyagers were Incessant In their expressions of surprise, joy, and admiration at the scenes of beauty and endless magnificence that every turn disclosed to their view. Untrodden forests descending down the long slopes, even to the water's edge, or crowning the towering cliffs; picturesque islands reposing in calm beauty on the surface of the river, still many miles wide; broad black portals, between which mighty streams poured in their deep, silent waters; furious torrents, descending from the upper country and tumbling down the rocky banks in sheets of foam:—these, the more striking features of the scenery, surrounded by lofty mountains whose peaks were visible in all directions, filled Casola with a painter's enthusiasm as he gazed on them with a painter's eye. "Glorious land!" he exclaimed; "what boundless treasures do thy vast rivers presage! If the toiling European only saw the riches thou art so lavish in displaying, dearly as he loves the home of his fathers, precious as he holds its memories, how soon would he abandon all, to dwell with thee and share thy birthright of freedom and abundance!"

Early in June the travellers landed at Quebec, the chief settlement in Canada; and Casola lost no time in calling on the Rev. Father Francis de la Valle, bishop of the diocese. In answer to his inquiries regarding the parts of the country in which Father de Seranne had been stationed, he learned that his missionary labors had been very widely extended. Many years ago, in company with Father Dreuillettes, he had penetrated into the Indian country that lay away far in the south towards the English settlements. From that country, in which he had been very successful, he was afterwards removed; and, Father Dreuillettes having died, the Indians of that place—the Abenakis, as they were called— were now under the spiritual care of Father Simon, who had established a mission on the Kennebeck River. Father de Seranne had been afterwards for a long time among the Iroquois and Hurons, and had spent several years in the region of the great lakes, in an unavailing attempt to ascertain the mysterious fate of Father René Mesnard, the first missionary that had ventured to penetrate the limitless tracts that lay in the remote West. As to the face which he had spoken of with so much emphasis, the good bishop had never heard of it, and what was thereby meant he could not even conjecture. Regarding its probable locality, of course, he could not furnish the slightest information himself; but he would refer Casola to a man who, if any one could be, was perfectly competent to give him every necessary information on the subject, or, if that was impossible, would put him on the most assured way to procure it.

This man's name was Jacques Clérêt; and Casola soon saw that the bishop's expressions in his favor had not exaggerated his merits. Since his arrival in the country, Jacques had led a wild, wandering, restless life,—exploring, hunting, trading, making incursions into the English and Dutch settlements, and often joining in the more numerous expeditions against the hostile and wily Iroquois. He had accompanied Marquette in his famous voyage down the Mississippi, and had been one of his attendants when that pious hero expired so tranquilly on the shores of the Algonquin Lake. He would have formed one of La Salle's party, at that time engaged in the farther exploration of the Mississippi; but at the time of their departure he was unable to move, owing to the effects of a wound received in the leg from the rifle of a prowling Iroquois, whom, however, he had contrived to capture and slay. He knew the Algonquin language, and was intimately acquainted with every variety of forest life.

Casola confessed to himself that, if mortal means were of any avail to assist him in his search, Jacques Clérêt was the best instrument for his purpose. Accordingly, he stated at once the object of his long voyage, and the grounds upon which he founded his hope of success. He detailed the exact words of De Seranne, as well as he could remember them from his mother's relation, and asked Jacques what he considered to be the meaning of the priest's expressions. Jacques listened to the whole story with great attention, occasionally surveying Casola with glances expressive of much interest. When the latter had finished, Jacques replied,—

"I knew Father de Seranne very well. Eighteen years ago he rescued me when on the point of being tortured to death by a party of Onondagas into whose power I had unluckily fallen. I went in his company as far as Lake Champlain, when I separated from him and returned home by the Iroquois River. He crossed the lake with the intention of paying a visit to the Abenakis, among whom he had previously dwelt, but whom he had been obliged to leave, in order to inquire into the probable fate of Father Mesnard. It was from this unsuccessful search that he was returning when he rescued me."

"Did he converse much with you?" asked Casola.

"Yes," replied Jacques. "I was the only Frenchman besides himself in the company; the rest were Indian converts. But our conversation was principally about his late expedition. I remember his also regretting that the savage nature of the Mohawks had been so much stimulated by the Dutch of New Netherlands, and that the life of a missionary was no longer safe among the most docile of the Five Nations. In order to secure themselves the monopoly of the fur-trade, they had supplied the natives with rum, taught them the use of fire-arms, and instigated them against the missionaries as against so many sorcerers."

"Have you ever seen him since?" was Casola's next question.

"No," replied Clérêt. "After that time I dwelt principally in the Huron country, till about ten years ago, when I settled in Fort Cataraqui (now called Fort Frontenac, from our present Governor), and there I remained until I started for the Mississippi along with Father Marquette."

"Could De Seranne have alluded to any thing he had seen in the Western country?"

"It is likely," replied Jacques, "that, if he had seen any thing of that nature out there, I would have heard of it. Long before I saw the mighty waterfall, I had known every one of its features by description."

"What waterfall?" asked Casola.

"The falls of the Unghiara," said Jacques. "You see that broad stream before you,— the St. Lawrence. At the great falls,

almost every drop contained in that river plunges down a precipice five hundred feet deep and a mile across."*

"Great Heavens! how grand!" cried Casola, in ecstasy at
the idea.

"Wait till you see them," said Jacques. "If you do not regard the risk of being scalped by the Mohawks, we will go and
see them before you return to your own country."

"I will sketch them," cried the painter.

"You will hardly succeed," said Jacques. "All the grandeur
proceeds from the vastness of the scene and the never-ending
resistless motion. These you can never present on canvas. Even
the accompaniments are sublime. I can never tell how I felt at
the first distant sight I caught of the clouds of spray swelling
up into the sky like the smoke of a burning forest."

After a few moments lost in thought, Casola roused himself, saying,— "But, time enough for that. We were speaking
of Father de Seranne."

"True," said Jacques. "I do not think he could have seen
anything like what you allude to in the Western country without my having heard of it. And yet, on our voyage down the
Mississippi, on the day before we came to the mouth of the
great river Pekitanoui (Missouri), I remember having seen
great wonders of which we had never been told. On the face of
high, steep rocks, far beyond the reach of human hands, we
distinctly saw the figures of two dreadful monsters, of red,
green, and blue colors, which upon a nearer approach we perceived were merely painted. The Indians who had directed us
as to the course we were to pursue knew nothing of them; and
we could not conceive how a painter could be got there skilful
enough to execute them, or even how he could possibly have
ascended the rock upon which he had painted them."

"Were they skilfully executed?" demanded Casola.

"With great skill," replied Jacques; "and Father Marquette
was as much surprised as any of us. However, we were then at

---

*This pardonable exaggeration as to the height of the Falls was gen-
erally prevalent long after Jacques's time.

least one hundred leagues distant from the nations that lived along the Algonquin Lake, and it is not surprising that they had not given us any information respecting them. But Father de Seranne had never been so far away as that. I have been in every part of the country in which he lived, except among the Abenakis."

"Have you been told of curiosities not so remarkable in their appearance as the Falls?" asked Casola.

"Yes; of many a one," was Jacques's reply. "For example, I do not know how often I have been told of the wonderful shapes presented by the great rocks on the southern shores of the Upper Lake. I can hardly doubt that what Father de Seranne has seen must be among the Abenakis: at all events, let us try *them* first."

"From all I can understand," observed Casola, "the difficulties of my search are only commencing now. But how can I think of asking you to share them?"

"Do not ask such a question," answered Jacques. "You have interested me exceedingly. I am very curious to see the end of your expedition. Besides, you cannot do without me. A stranger can scarcely travel fifty yards here without a guide."

"But, then, the danger, the remuneration—"

"As for the danger," said Jacques, "our ways of regarding things are quite different. I have been a forester for nearly twenty years. An unfortunate incident, to which it is not now necessary to make further allusion, drove me over here in my nineteenth year, when Montagny was Governor. A few years afterwards, the object of my affections followed me, and I led a happy life for nearly ten years, when, on my return from a profitable fur expedition, I found that during my absence a party of Mohawks had invaded Quebec by night, burned many houses, and murdered many women and children. My wife and child were among the number; and from that day to this, danger has had no terrors for me. As to remuneration, thanks to my experience in the fur-trade, I am now a rich man. Regarding the trouble, the truth is, since I have missed La Salle's expedition to the Mississippi, and as war has ceased, or appeared to cease, I have nothing particular to do, and I feel the time hanging very heavily on my hands. Indeed, I had almost formed the resolution of spending the remaining few years of my life in the Jesuit Seminary as a Lay Brother. So, no more objections, I will only be too happy to accompany you. Let me make all the preparations. We will start tomorrow."

CHAPTER VII.

THE JOURNEY.

THE UNEXPECTED difficulties which Casola encountered in his journey seem to have prevented him from being very full in his details. Though his geographical observations are generally accurate enough, yet his description of scenery is sometimes rather vague, and it is not always easy to recognize the exact spot on the route to which allusion is made. In recording his impressions of American scenery, he relied mainly on his pencil, his written remarks being mostly confined to the more prominent features.

Early on the following morning, Casola was called upon by Jacques, who told him that, every thing being now ready for their departure, longer delay was unnecessary. Delighted at this despatch, he was ready in a few minutes to start on his exciting expedition. Descending the steep slopes of Cape Diamond until he came to the river, he found there two birch canoes in charge of the four Abenaki Indians who were to be their guides. Complete preparations had indeed been made, short as the time had been, and Casola beheld with surprise and pleasure the stores of provisions, the blankets, and other facilities for encampment, with which, besides six long guns, the birches were supplied. Jacques presented Casola with a pair of pistols, a long hunting-knife, and a gun, which the latter found no difficulty afterwards in carrying through the woods, as his painting apparatus was confined to some pasteboard and pencils. Jacques, Casola, and an Indian took one boat, the remaining three Indians the other, and all pushed quickly up the stream. The Indians were tall, muscular men, almost entirely naked, and with what seemed to Casola a singularly wild and savage expression of countenance.

He said as much to Jacques.

"Oh," said the latter, "the Abenakis, though very brave warriors when once aroused, are of a comparatively mild and peaceful disposition. They belong to the Algonquin tribe, and they are women when compared to the Iroquois. The Iroquois are the most cruel and vindictive of all the Indians. Before we return, you will have opportunities enough to verify this."

"Does our road lie near the lands of the Iroquois?" asked Casola.

"No," replied Jacques; "but we shall probably have to return that way. The Indians tell me that the most direct road to their country, though in some places very difficult, is not tedious. This road, which lies almost due south, we will follow; for, as we do not know how long our search is to last, our object at present is to be sparing of time. The other route, by which the Abenaki country is entered from the west, we may probably follow on our return to Quebec. Though it is longer, it is altogether free from those high mountains which, like those on our present route, in winter are covered with snow, and are extremely difficult, if not quite impossible, to cross."

"How far is it to the Abenaki country?"

"More than a hundred leagues."

"It will not take us till winter to travel a hundred leagues."

"The Indians tell me we shall be often quite satisfied if we make a league a day."

Thus conversing, they paddled up the St. Lawrence. They soon crossed the stream, and, entering the mouth of a large river flowing into it from the south, which Jacques called the Chaudière, they ascended its course for many days. On the first day, Casola enjoyed a sight of much grandeur. After several hours' sailing on smooth waters overhung by trees of gigantic growth, the silence of the forest was broken by a sound as of the rising wind. This gradually increased in distinctness, until he could easily recognize the roar of falling waters; the current over which they sailed grew more and more turbid, when a sudden turn revealed the magnificent cause. Over the edge of a rocky wall one hundred and fifty feet in perpendicular height, the impetuous Chaudière precipitated its foaming waters. The line of the edge was broken by huge beetling rocks which divided the torrent into three distinct falls, that were, however, again united long before they reached the boiling gulf. Black, craggy precipices lined the sides of the white cataract, whilst far above, on each side of the rushing flood, the eternal forest reposed in motionless serenity. It was a picture perfect in all its details.

Casola could not restrain his transport.

"Yes," said Jacques, "they are very grand. They are not, indeed, half as high as the falls on the St. Charles, nor in vastness of proportion can they be at all compared to the sea that plunges down at Unghiara; but they are more complete than either. Here we are shut out from every other view. With nothing but water beneath, forest around, and sky above us, these falling waters impress us with all their charms. Nothing extraneous breaks in to mar the effect. I like to be here: nowhere else do I feel more calm. I have often been here before; but at every fresh visit I still find a new charm."

Casola looked at Jacques, as he spoke, with a thoughtful expression, but continued silent. But now they had to land and carry their boats, provisions, guns, and camp-equipage through the woods for about half a mile to the navigable waters above. This they could do with the greatest ease as the boats were of such light construction than an Indian found no difficulty in carrying one altogether on his own shoulders. These boats excited Casola's surprise by their great effectiveness notwithstanding the simplicity of their construction. They consisted of a slight but strong framework, long and narrow in shape, and a covering of bark taken whole from the birch-tree. They were impervious to water except where it oozed in through the joinings, and rocks did them little harm. Casola often saw them shooting down rapids with perfect safety, where boats of less frail material would infallibly have been swamped. Their journey at first was very pleasant and easy. During the day their birches glided swiftly up the smooth stream, and at night, moored to some projecting tree and strewn with furs and blankets, they proved luxurious beds. The trout and other savory fish, which the Indians speared with marvellous ease, imparted an agreeable relish to the coarse but palatable provisions, of which they had laid in a plentiful supply at Quebec. The profound stillness and savage grandeur of the wilderness that enclosed the waters over which they sailed, appear to have made a deep impression on Casola. His imagination delighted to plunge into the mysterious depths of those dark forests, where so many countless generations of leaves had mouldered away in silence, never displaced by the foot of man.

Obstacles to their progress, however, soon began to appear. Sometimes they came to a part of the river where, from a contraction of the rocky banks, the current flowed with such impetuosity that it was impossible to stem it. Sometimes after a sail of many hours on smooth water, they came in sight of a sloping ledge of rocks in the river's bed, over which the furious waters rushed, whirling and boiling and covered with foam. The labor through which they had to go until they could discover navigable water began by degrees also to become extremely difficult. The forest generally extended to the water's edge, and the growth of underwood was often so thick that, in order to pass at all, the travellers sometimes found it necessary to spend a whole day in cutting themselves a path with their axes.

Their route, which had hitherto been in a valley, now began to ascend. Swifter and swifter became the course of the stream, and the rapids grew so frequent that at last the Indians pronounced the river no longer practicable. The birches being now useless, Casola expected to see them abandoned; but he was told that, as soon as the highlands separating the tributaries of the St. Lawrence from those of the ocean were crossed, they would again become indispensable. Their progress for several days after this was very slow. The route lay among dense woods, through which they had continually to cut their way. The path was often so steep that the feet of one traveller were on a level with the head of his successor. Nor were they without company in these gloomy solitudes. Sometimes a sudden rattle told them of the dangerous neighborhood of a deadly snake, which, however, was perhaps as much frightened as themselves. Sometimes a wildcat would cross their path with stealthy footsteps. Often they were startled by the angry howl of the wolf; and occasionally the surly bear would be seen for a moment surveying the intruders with no welcoming glance, and then disappearing in the recesses of the dark wood.

As they ascended higher, the cold became severe and their labor seemed endless. Snow lay deep in many places, and thus increased the other difficulties of the journey. Over frosts, snows, rocks, and decayed timber they had now to make their way; and, as Casola could not see the least sign of a road, and the sun was often wholly concealed by the dark clouds, he could not help admiring the unerring certainty with which the Indians went forward. They never turned to the right or left, nor even paused to ascertain their further course. This confidence, Jacques said, was owing to certain observations they had made regarding which side of the trees the moss grew on, and also the direction taken by some of the branches. Jacques was a very cheerful companion. He not only seemed to disregard the labor himself, but succeeded in making his companions likewise forget it. He evidently had conceived a great affection for Casola, which he showed by a multitude of kind attentions. He cooked his meals, chose the best place around the fire for him to lie at nights, spoke about his mother and the picture, told him all kinds of Indian legends and wild adventures of his own among the savages, helped him with his stout arm when the way was more than ordinarily rough, and, if his spirits were gloomy, brightened them up with the recital of jests and merry tales, and often trolled out, with a good voice, some gay song learned long ago in "la belle France." This last means was always effectual in cheering up Casola, who, besides possessing a fine voice and a good ear, was very fond of music. When Jacques burst out into some merry lay, Casola would pick up the air at once, join his friend in the chorus, or make verses himself, as the case might be; and thus they would sing and sing, to the manifest delight of the Indians, until the old forests rang again. Casola, however, remarked that, twice or three times during the journey, Jacques himself became silent and gloomy, as if he were a prey to mournful recollections. On such occasions he made every effort to arouse his friend, and he was always successful.

They soon began to descend; but the stream whose course they now followed was as yet of no further importance than to show them the way. They had heretofore travelled almost directly south; but Casola now remarked that their course lay nearly due east. Lofty mountains towered on each side; and, as the travellers wound down the deep gorges of these highlands, Casola was never weary of admiring the great ocean of forest that lay before him, spread out in all directions. One day he was assured by one of the Indians that the faint white streak, which he could scarcely detect on the verge of the horizon, was the great sea that separated him from his own country. After nearly a whole day's toil in descending the mountains, the stream becoming comparatively smooth and deep, they could once more launch their canoes on its waters. But this was only a momentary relief; for they soon landed on its southern bank, and, taking up the boats, once more plunged directly into the forest. Here Casola thought he could detect a kind of path that led south; yet he felt this to be one of the worst spots on the whole journey. The undergrowth was dense and luxuriant, the ground was soft, and in many places so swampy that they often found it necessary to fell a tree in order to make a bridge over the broad pools of black, slimy ooze. This difficult march, however, was not of long duration. Ere the last faint trace of daylight had altogether disappeared before the mild rays of the full moon, now rising bright and cloudless in the eastern sky, the travellers found themselves on the northern shores of a great lake, the Indian name for which, though Casola heard it, he did not remember. Here they rested for the night;

and, while some commenced preparing the boats for the morning's journey, others busied themselves in getting ready the evening meal. A most welcome addition was made to their feast through the skill of Jacques. His keen eye had caught sight of a fine moose that was descending to the lake-shore to drink, and his unerring bullet laid low the antlered monarch of the forest. Casola was surprised at the size of the animal. Its body he considered as big as a horse's, and much larger than that of any stag he had ever seen in Europe. The flesh was tender and savory, but he thought it more resembled beef than venison.

The greater part of next day was spent on the lake, though the Indians drove their boats forward with great rapidity, as the waters were smooth and deep. Here again Casola took occasion to admire the wild grandeur of the ever-changing scenery. Now the canoes swept round rocky cliffs, now they wound through the countless islands, and now they emerged into the sparkling waters, where the lake expanded so widely that every sign of the shore was altogether lost on one side. At other times their course was so hemmed in on all sides by the gloomy forest, that outlet in any direction seemed impossible. Oh, the grandeur of that dark, impenetrable forest,—silent forest, where no song of birds ever broke the brooding stillness,—opaque forest, shutting out, like a prison-wall, the view in all directions except on the northwest, where the whole background was filled up with lofty mountains, whose dim, faint summits hardly formed a line on the bright azure!

Towards evening they reached the southern extremity of the lake, from the west side of which they saw its waters issue forth in a broad stream, deep and rapid. Into this they immediately entered; and, following its course, except where falls or violent rapids intervened, they found themselves by the close of the next day approaching the little Indian town of Norrigevocque.*

---

* The route of Arnold's famous expedition through the same wilderness, made nearly a century later, seems to have been more obstructed than this of Casola's, and to have deviated little less from a straight line.

CHAPTER VIII.

THE INDIAN VILLAGE.

THIS SETTLEMENT was situated on the Kennebeck River, at that point where, meeting a smaller stream from the south, it turned off at right angles to the east. The huts—of which the general plan was a frame of poles meeting above and covered with bark—were scattered here and there without any attempt at regularity. High above them all towered the little chapel, of more artful construction and ornamented with a belfry. Just as they were entering the borders of the village, the bell rang out, sweet and loud, the evening call to the "*Ave Maria.*" The sounds were so unexpected, the very idea of the gentle prayer, commemorative of the Incarnation, ascending to heaven out of the depths of that wild forest, was in itself so startling, that for an instant Casola could hardly help thinking that his ears were deceived. But the sight of Jacques and the Indians piously bending whilst they repeated the prayer, assured him of the reality of the sounds that now died away sweetly on the evening air.

They were welcomed with much joy by the Indians. Jacques and Casola had one of the best lodges of the village assigned to their use, and their companions, who, though they belonged to the same tribe, were entire strangers there, were treated with every hospitality. They soon learned that they had come too late to see Father Simon. A few days before, he had set out to visit another settlement of Indians, on the banks of a great river farther east, and the period of his return was quite uncertain. Somewhat disconcerted at this intelligence, Jacques, at whose instigation Casola had undertaken the present long and toilsome journey, proposed that they should start next morning for the eastern settlement; for, without some new information obtained from Father Simon's own lips, he thought they could proceed no farther. However, having conversed for a long time with some of the oldest Indians of the village in their own language, he learned enough to change his determination; and, appearing next morning before Casola with a joyful countenance, he said that so far every thing had been quite successful, and that the object of their expedition was likely to be accomplished very soon. To Casola's most eager inquiries he would give no further information, unwilling to excite too highly expectations which after all might be disappointed, but told him that, after a few days' rest, they would resume their journey.

To Casola this resting-time passed very quickly. He spent it in observing the various phases of Indian life, which he contemplated with much interest. He saw much to admire. His European ideas of savage life had led him to expect quite a different scene. In a village containing several hundred inhabitants he found perfect order and discipline prevailing. There was no court, prison, or punishment of any kind. All—from the oldest sagamore to the youngest infant that tumbled about before the huts—lived in perfect freedom, and yet the rights of others were scrupulously respected. The clearings around the village produced abundance of maize, turnsols, pompions, and other vegetables; for since the arrival of the Jesuits among them their knowledge of agriculture had been greatly extended. Whilst the men fought their enemies, or went on hunting expeditions, killing wild animals for their fur or their flesh, the women attended to the domestic affairs, cultivated the ground, reaped the corn, and underwent the most laborious employments, with perfect good will and apparent happiness; for Casola always saw them laughing, bustling busily about, and talking with great loquacity. The men, on the contrary, he considered very grave and silent in their deportment. Unless when engaged in their sterner occupations, he saw them lead an indolent—perhaps a tiresome —life. It was only what he expected to hear, when he was told that, notwithstanding all Father Simon's instructions, their hearts still panted for war. Of the peace which they had concluded with the English several years before, on terms very honorable to themselves, they were now heartily weary. Several acts of the late war still rankled in their bosoms; their enemies provoked them daily by new acts of invasion and injustice; and Casola saw that few years could elapse before hostilities would burst out anew with greater animosity than ever.

Still, he was delighted to see the fervor with which they performed their religious exercises. Three times a day almost all the inhabitants of the village proceeded to the little chapel, where, in the absence of Father Simon, prayers were said and instructions given by a venerable chieftain who had been one of the earliest converts to Christianity. The same patriarch took care of the little school, which the children attended regularly every day. Their apprehensions being naturally quick, the progress they had made in their humble studies, though they wanted many of the most indispensable articles of civilized school-rooms, was quite enough to surprise Casola. This he ascertained by personal examination; for most of the young pupils had acquired some knowledge of the French language. When he told them the name of his country, one little fellow, sketching a rude map of Italy on the floor, and making a large dot in the middle to represent Rome, asked him if he knew what *that* was, and if he had often seen their Holy Father. Their love for Father Simon approached veneration. They always spoke of him with the utmost affection and respect; and their eyes glistened with tears at the idea of his return. They were merry, lively creatures, inoffensive, if not courteous, in their conduct, easily amused, and they hardly ever quarreled. They soon formed an intimacy with Jacques, who told them wonderful stories in their own language; but a few pencil-portraits of the elders, and some groups of the children at their amusements, in which the features of each were easily recognized, rendered Casola immediately the object of universal regard and admiration.

CHAPTER IX.

THE DISCOVERY.

UT IT was now time to resume their journey. As the return of Father Simon might not occur for several months, Jacques and Casola had to depart without seeing him, being desirous to bring their expedition to a conclusion before the cold weather should set in. On the morning of their departure, the Indians, young and old, crowded round them, testifying much affection; and six young men of the village insisted on being allowed to accompany them, besides the two that had been already appointed for that purpose. They followed the course of the river already spoken of as having entered the Kennebeck on the south, and ascended its waters for nearly twenty miles. Now, for the first time, Casola began to trace distinctly the outlines of a towering range of mountains, which were so whitish in their appearance that he had hitherto considered them vast piles of mist. He was informed by one of his new companions, named Toxas, that they were called the "White Foreheads," and considered to be the homes of mighty spirits, and that his course lay directly at their base. When they came to a part of the river where it turned to the north, they left it, and, shouldering their boats, plunged into the woods and followed a southerly direction for a few hours. After a portage, which was not very difficult, they came to the banks of a river much larger, deeper, and more rapid than the one they had left. Up this new stream—called by the Indians *"Amariscoggine"*—they now ascended, their course being almost due west: and they soon found themselves encircled by lofty mountains. Still they followed up the rocky channel, where the stream was sometimes deep and smooth, often narrow, rapid, and precipitous, for two days, until they came at last to a sudden bend where this river likewise wheeled off to the north. Leaving it, and concealing their boats in the windings of the rocky banks, they waded for some distance up the waters of a small rivulet, when a sudden clearing away of the thick forest revealed to Casola a view of the grandest mountain-scenery he had witnessed since his arrival in the country.

A vast valley, at least twenty miles long, and of varying breadths, lay stretched between two ranges of mountains, which rose tall, dark, and frowning on each side. On the right, in particular, he remarked three peaks, which could not be less than a mile in perpendicular height; and behind, soaring far above them in silent majesty, rose the bald dome of another mountain,—the king of his companions,—his white summit scarcely distinguishable from the fleecy clouds that sailed round it in the bright sky. High up their sides climbed the dark forest in densest masses, except where interrupted by white streaks, which he was told were vast spots, miles in width, bare and sterile, marking the track of the thundering avalanche that had been plunged down by some sudden loosening of the rocky surface, with resistless might, from the precipitous cliffs above. These were the "White Foreheads;" and on the other side lay the object of their long search. But, according to the Indians, no one could ascend these mountains and live. Christianity had by no means removed the ideas of fear and reverence with which they had been always regarded. They were, they said, the abodes of powerful spirits, the masters of thunder, lightning, storms, and rain, who often fought and made these summits their battle-grounds. These were the appropriate theatres for the dread encounters of those jealous spirits; for in that region the clouds could dash together, the winds roar, the lightnings flash, and the thunders rattle with all their fury, without one sound of the mighty conflict ever reaching mortal ear. Some daring hunters, having presumed to pursue moose-deer that had retired up these mountains for refuge, had never returned, and their fate was never known.

The travellers continued to pursue their southerly course on foot through the valley, ascending by one stream, descending by another, until, meeting a third that flowed from the west, they pursued it up towards its source. It led them into defiles that wound round the base of the great ridge; but they soon got so completely entangled in this mountain-circle that Casola saw no possibility of an escape from his position except by climbing those dreaded dizzy heights. But the ridge that lies before them is thousands of feet high, and so steep that it is perhaps impossible to climb it. Still he sees the Indians pursue their way without apprehension. They ascend the stream with perfect confidence. He follows them; and, after struggling for some hours through the dense forest, a sudden opening of the woods affords him a glimpse of a magnificent spectacle.

Rising to thousands of feet on each side, he beholds the walls of an enormous cleft in the mountain, extending from summit to base, as if the mighty ridge had first split asunder and then wheeled apart, like folding-doors, in order to allow him a passage. He even fancied that if these precipitous cliffs were to roll together once more, his eye could detect the precise spots where the corresponding projections and cavities would exactly meet. This valley was at first about a quarter of a mile wide, the stream still making its way through the rocks that encumbered its bottom; but, as the travellers ascended, it gradually became narrower, until at last the walls were hardly twenty feet apart, although they still rose high and perpendicular. The millions of workmen, thought Casola, that had erected the Pyramids, were they to labor at it for a hundred years, could not cut so perfect a road through the heart of those mighty mountains.

Thus escaping from their giant prison, they journeyed onwards, and soon struck on a wild river, which the Indians called the "Amonousuque," flowing westerly in a rapid stream. This they followed with much difficulty; for the valley through which it flowed was very narrow, and the forest as dense as ever. At last, leaving it and ascending higher ground, they saw the summits of the "White Foreheads," now many miles behind them, reflecting the last rays of the setting sun, whilst a heavy shadow lay on the intervening forest. Here they encamped for the night, weary of their wilderness journey, but in better spirits than ever; for next day was to fulfil the promise of their Indian friends.

Resuming their journey early next morning, they proceeded directly south; and, upon approaching another mountain-chain, they were admitted into its interior by an entrance of the same magnificent and wonderful character as that by which they had lately made their egress. As before, it seemed as if these frowning mountains, like mighty sliding portals, had been drawn aside to afford the travellers an entrance to the wonders that lay concealed within.

Now that Casola was drawing near the end of his journey, when the object of his hopes and fears was almost within his grasp, he felt himself becoming all at once uneasy and anxious. What if it proved a mere chimera, after all? Might it not be some pious but weak fancy of good Father de Seranne or the childish object of some Indian superstition? Rapidly as the decisive moment approached, he often wished it were over and the suspense under which he labored ended. But no such thoughts found place in Jacques's breast. He even confessed that in the feelings of awe and reverence with which the Indians approached the spot he himself fully shared.

On they hurried now with accelerated footsteps in the dark forest, through whose dense foliage they occasionally discerned the wooded cliffs and grim precipices that overhung their path. On still they hurried, until, coming to a little lake, Casola and Jacques halted on its shores, in obedience to a signal of the Indians, who continued to advance along its left bank. When they had gone about half-way, the leader, Toxas, stopped, turned round, looked over the lake, and then, raising his left arm, nodded to his white companions to look in the direction which he indicated. Breathless with expectation, they hurried up, gave one glance, and Casola, with a cry, acknowledged that his wish was at last attained.

From the other side of the little lake rose a mountain, steep and dark, and clothed with forest nearly to its summit. On the right the ridge sloped away gradually, and its outline was soon lost with its neighbors; but on the left the bare rock rose out of the dark forest, five hundred feet high, and perpendicular as a wall. More than half-way up this wall, and extending nearly to the top, Casola saw the features of a vast face, calm and stern in aspect, sharply defined against the blue sky. The forehead, nose, lips, and chin were evidently immense blocks of stone; but they were so disposed and fitted to each other as to form the outline of a human countenance, not only perfectly correct in all its proportions, but revealing a sternness and majesty of expression that completely enchanted him. There, on the summit of a mountain, among the clouds as it were, fully a mile distant, hung the portrait, the august features of which had so long haunted his imagination, waking and sleeping, as

The Profile. Moses F. Sweetser. *Views of the White Mountain,* Boston, 1879. From the author's collection.

those of the Divine Judge, but which he had heretofore been so unsuccessful in his endeavors to represent. For a long time he continued to gaze on it with intense rapture.

Jacques also looked at the wonderful Face with feelings of indescribable awe, and listened with the liveliest interest to the Indians as they recorded the various changes of expression it had assumed in the course of ages. Formerly, said they, before the white man made his appearance, it seemed happy, and looked with benign and gracious aspect out over the wild forests where the aborigines chased the deer and slew the savage bear. At certain times every year, the little lake was a rendezvous where deputies from various parts of the country—even from the distant Western lakes—met, bringing presents to testify their gratitude to the great "*Onon-manito*," or "*mountain spirit*," for the produce of their land, the success of the chase, or the increasing prosperity, in general, of each tribe.

But in progress of time the old man remarked, with disquietude, that the Face began to lose its joyful expression, and to assume an appearance of grief, which they feared omened some unspeakable misfortune that was to befall the nation. Full of alarm, they had sought to propitiate it with prayers and sacrifices and new treaties of peace (for they might have offended it by their frequent wars); but, to their utter consternation, they saw it becoming every year more and more stern and inexorable in its lineaments, though it still preserved that mournful expression which had excited their alarm at first. "And ever since," added Toxas, gloomily, "it is becoming sterner and more relentless; and our oldest sages affirm that, notwithstanding the efforts made by the good French *Blackrobes* to introduce Christianity among us, this continued change only forebodes the utter annihilation of the Indian race and name, and that the day of our doom is fast approaching."

Whilst the Indians thus related the sad presentiments inspired by the wonderful Face, Casola was taking his sketch, though, as he afterwards told Jacques, that was a needless operation; for the majestic outlines of those features had engraved themselves imperishably on the tablets of his memory forever.

The manuscript life did not conclude here. It contained a description of Casola's visits to the Falls and the great Lakes, and some singular adventures that befell him there. It also detailed some surprising incidents in Jacques's life, which united the friends more closely together, and induced Jacques to return to Europe with Casola, at whose house in Acqua Chiara he spent the rest of his days. It told how Casola found his mother still living, how he painted his great picture, which she had the happiness to see and enjoy many a year before her death. But it was the next day that I learned all these additional circumstances. As soon as my curiosity respecting the origin of the picture was gratified, I preferred spending the remainder of the night in writing out the principal points in the strange story thus related, and indulging in the reverie to which they naturally led. Of course, long before I came to the catastrophe, I had known what it was to be. An early familiarity with the famous New Hampshire Mountains permitted no uncertainty on that point, and enabled me to acknowledge the general correctness of Casola's statements; making due allowance, of course, for all the difficulties under which he had labored. His other adventures in America may perhaps furnish matter for a future paper.

THE END.

The Golden Era

Guidebooks & History

The Profile House

Profile, Franconia Notch. Illustration from a 19th Century Souvenir Book. From the Author's collection.

GUIDEBOOKS & HISTORY

The Profile Mountain in New Hampshire
Gen. Martin Field

General Martin Field's description of the Old Man of the Mountain, appearing in the July 1828 edition of *The American Journal of Science and Arts*, edited by Benjamin Silliman, is the earliest known account of the Profile. Field, born in 1773 in either Leverett or Everett, Massachusetts, attended Williams College and then studied at Dartmouth College. He was an attorney who practiced law in New Fane (now Newfane), Vermont. He studied the geology of Vermont and New Hampshire after he retired.

O Professor Silliman.
Nov. 22, 1827

Dear Sir:

On a late excursion, which I made among the White Mountains in New Hampshire, I visited Franconia and the Profile Mountain, which has long been considered a rare phenomenon.

I there procured a sketch of the mountain, which I enclose to you, and if it meets your approbation, you will please to insert it in the Journal of Science, &c.

I am sir, very respectfully, yours &c.

Martin Field

New Fane, Vt.

NOTICE OF THE PROFILE MOUNTAIN IN NEW HAMPSHIRE

The White Mountain range passes through the easterly part of Franconia, and presents numerous elevations and sublime mountain scenery. But the greatest elevation in that vicinity, is Mount La Fayette, which forms the northern boundary of the *Notch*, so called, and is supposed to exceed four thousand feet, in height. The Profile Mountain is nigh the road leading from Franconia to Plymouth—is five miles from the lower iron works, in Franconia, and about three miles south of Mount La Fayette. The elevation of this mountain, I understand, has never been accurately ascertained, but it is generally estimated to be, at least, one thousand feet. The road passes very nigh the foot of the mountain, from which it rises abruptly, at an angle of about 80° to the profile rock. The bare rock, on which the profile is delineated, is granite, and having been long exposed to the atmosphere, its color is a dark reddish brown. A side view of the projecting rock, near the peak of the mountain, in a northern direction, exhibits the profile of the human face, in which every line and feature are conspicuous. But after passing the mountain to the south, the likeness is immediately lost.

Notes of a Tour in the United States and Canada in the Summer and Autumn of 1847

Jabez Burns

The very name, "The Old Man of the Mountain" may have its origins in the 1840s when Nathaniel Peabody Rogers, a leader of the anti-slave movement in New Hampshire, edited a small paper in Concord called the *Herald of Freedom*. When Rogers wrote about the scenery of his native state he signed the articles *Old Man of the Mountain*, a name that he reportedly had applied to the Profile in Franconia Notch. During the summer of 1847 another abolitionist, Jabez Burns, visited New Hampshire and saw the Profile. Burns, born in 1805 in Oldham, Lancashire, England, was first a bookseller and then a Baptist minister in London. He wrote a large number of religious books and in 1847 was a delegate from England to the Free Will Baptists Meeting held in the United States. After the meeting Burns took a trip throughout the country speaking against slavery. Burns' short book, *Notes of a Tour in the United States and Canada in the Summer and Autumn of 1847* was published in London in 1848. In the introduction to his book Burns wrote: "Let that foul stain of Slavery be removed from the United States, and then she will rise to the noblest altitude among the nations of the earth." After a night in Littleton, New Hampshire, Burns traveled by stage through Franconia Notch and described his trip as follows:

HE NEXT DAY I was conducted by Elder Blake in his private conveyance a distance of 40 miles to Holderness Village.

This is considered one of the finest rides in America. A few miles above Franconia we passed through the Notch, a narrow opening between two lofty mountains, in which nature appears in its most awful grandeur. On the summit of one of these towering Cliffs there is a most striking and remarkable profile, called "The Old Man of the Mountain." The face is perfect, and travellers in the summer season come hundreds of miles to see it, and the wild scenery that surrounds it. The old man's head is often enveloped in mist, but we were so happy as to have a bright and clear day, so that our view was most perfect. What is also remarkable in this object of universal attention, is that as you proceed a few yards farther, the profile is changed, and the face appears like that of a long, thin faced old woman. The face might now pass as that of the Granny of the last hundred generations.

Scenery of the White Mountains
William Oakes

Scenery of the White Mountains by William Oakes, published in 1848, has long been regarded as one of the finest White Mountain picture books. Oakes, born in Danvers, Massachusetts, in 1799, was educated as a lawyer at Harvard. However, after a visit to the White Mountains in 1825 he became fascinated with the rare plant life found there and he abandoned his legal training in favor of work in botany. Shortly after his book was accepted for publication he died in an unexplained drowning accident off a Boston ferry boat. Included in the book were illustrations by Isaac Sprague and Godfrey Frankenstein. (*Scenery of the White Mountains* has been re-printed in several editions and may be available in bookstores.)

THE PROFILE ROCK

THE PROFILE ROCK is perhaps the greatest object of popular curiosity and admiration in the vicinity of the White Mountains. It has most of the features of the human face, forehead, eyebrows, nose, mouth, and chin; and though rough hewn by the hand of Time, they are all well proportioned to each other. It is hung up for exhibition in a most conspicuous and convenient situation, in bold relief against the sky, and in excellent contrast and harmony with the surrounding scenery.

The expression is severe and somewhat melancholy, and although there is a little feebleness about the mouth, on the whole, the face of the "Old Man of the Mountain" is set, and his countenance fixed and firm. He neither blinks at the near flashes of the lightning beneath his nose, nor flinches from the driving snow and sleet of the Franconia winter, which makes the very mercury of the thermometer shrink into the bulb and congeal.

Profile Mountain at Franconia, New Hampshire. Isaac Sprague. Included in *Scenery of the White Mountains* by William Oakes, Boston, 1848. From the author's collection.

The Profile is composed of three separate masses of rock, one of which forms the forehead, the second the nose and upper lip, and the third the chin. They are only brought into their proper position at a certain distance and place, which is on the well-travelled road through the Franconia Notch. It is about a quarter of a mile south of the Hotel, and is pointed out by a guide-board at the road-side.

Historical Relics of the White Mountains
John Hubbard Spaulding

John Hubbard Spaulding's *Historical Relics of the White Mountains*, published in 1855, was the first combination guide book and history of the White Mountains. Spaulding, born in Lancaster, New Hampshire, on August 17, 1821, was adopted by his aunt and uncle after his parents died when he was only three years old. After receiving a simple education in the local schools he both taught in the schools and worked on a farm. Later as a land surveyor he worked in Pittsburg, New Hampshire, to establish the border between the United States and Canada after the Webster and Ashburton Treaty was signed in 1842. Spaulding was an early explorer of the White Mountains, assisted in the construction of the Tip-Top House on the summit of Mt. Washington in 1853, and was later the manager of that building. In February 1862 Spaulding was a member of the first group to climb Mount Washington in the winter. One history of Coos County described Spaulding as follows: "He is a man of cultivation and literary taste, and a very ready, racy writer."

THE OLD MAN of the Mountain is a profile of the human face, situated on a peak of solid rock one thousand feet high, and nearly perpendicular from "*Ferrin's Pond*," known as the "*old man's washbowl*." This profile was discovered about forty years ago, while a party was laying out the road that passes it; and a guide-board directs the travellers attention thitherward. This likeness is produced by the irregular projection of five blocks of granite. Its semblance is quite lifelike, and is truly a worthy object of wonder. Various Indian utensils and relics have been found in that vicinity, which inclines to the belief that this with the aborigines was an object of superstitious homage. A footpath from the Lafayette House leads directly over the top of the old man's head, and sometimes a mortal may be seen standing among the bristly hair (bushes) of the old man's foretop. The entire height of this profile is sixty feet.

The White Hills
The Reverend Thomas Starr King

When it was published in 1859, The Reverend Thomas Starr King's *The White Hills: Their Legends, Landscape and Poetry* quickly became a popular history and guide to the White Mountains. Born in New York City in 1824, King and his family, his father a Universalist minister, soon moved to Portsmouth, New Hampshire, where he received his education in a private school before the family moved to Boston. After his father died when he was fifteen, King educated himself and supported his mother and the rest of his family. At the age of 19, he was teaching school in Medford, Massachusetts. Beginning in 1853, King wrote a series of letters for the Boston *Evening Transcript* describing his walks and drives in New Hampshire. These letters, written in King's very distinct style and prose, were to become his book about the White Mountains. In 1860 King moved to San Francisco and began his work with the Unitarian Church that was forming there. He quickly became a respected lecturer and orator in his newly adopted home where his positions on patriotism, the union, and liberty contributed to California remaining a free state during the debate over slavery. King died in 1864 while planning a book on the mountains of California. A statue in San Francisco and a mountain in Yosemite National Park honor King in California, while in New Hampshire, King Ravine, Mount Starr King, the Starr King Grange and the Starr King Cemetery remember this early explorer and writer about the White Mountains.

THE PEMIGEWASSET VALLEY

THE MOST ATTRACTIVE advertisement of the Franconia Notch to the travelling public is the rumor of the "Great Stone Face," that hangs upon one of its highest cliffs. If its enclosing walls were less grand, and its water gems less lovely, travellers would be still, perhaps, as strongly attracted to the spot, that they might see a mountain which breaks into human expression,—a piece of sculpture older than the Sphynx,—an intimation of the human countenance, which is the crown of all beauty, that was pushed out from the coarse strata of New England thousands of years before Adam.

The marvel of this countenance, outlined so distinctly against the sky at an elevation of nearly fifteen hundred feet above the road, is greatly increased by the fact that it is composed of three masses of rock which are not in perpendicular line with each other. On the brow of the mountain itself, standing on the visor of the helmet that covers the face, or directly underneath it on the shore of the little lake, there is no intimation of any human features in the lawless rocks. Remove but a few rods either way from the guide-board on the road, where you are advised to look up, and the charm is dissolved....

One of Mr. Hawthorne's admirable "Twice-told Tales" has woven a charming legend and moral about this mighty Profile; and in his description of the face the writer tells us: "It seemed as if an enormous giant, or Titan, had sculptured his own likeness on the precipice. There was the broad arch of the forehead, a hundred feet in height; the nose, with its long bridge; and the vast lips, which, if they could have spoken, would have rolled their thunder accents from one end of the valley to the other." We must reduce the scale of the charming story-teller's description. The whole profile is about eighty feet in length; and of the three separate masses of rock which are combined in its composition, one forms the forehead, another the nose and upper lip, and the third the chin. The best time to see the Profile is about four in the afternoon of a summer day. Then, standing by the little lake at the base and looking up, one fulfils the appeal of our great transcendental poet in a literal sense in looking at the jutting rocks, and,

> through their granite seeming
> Sees the smile of reason beaming.

The expression is really noble, with a suggestion partly of fatigue and melancholy. He seems to be waiting for some visitor or message. On the front of the cliff there is a pretty plain picture of a man with a pack on his back, who seems to be endeavoring to go up the valley. Perhaps it is the arrival of this arrested messenger that the old stone visage has been expecting for ages. The upper portion of the mouth looks a little weak, as though the front teeth had decayed, and the granite lip had consequently fallen in. Those who can see it with a thundercloud behind, and the slaty scud driving thin across it, will carry away the grandest impression which it ever makes on the beholder's mind. But when, after an August shower, late in the afternoon, the mists that rise from the forest below congregate around it, and, smitten with sunshine, break as they drift against its nervous outline, and hiding the mass of the mountain which it overhangs, isolate it with a thin halo, the countenance, awful but benignant, is "as if a mighty angel were sitting among the hills, and enrobing himself in a cloud vesture of gold and purple."

The whole mountain from which the Profile starts is one of the noblest specimens of majestic rock that can be seen in New Hampshire. One may tire of the craggy countenance sooner than of the sublime front and vigorous slopes of Mount Cannon itself—especially as it is seen, with its great patches of tawny color, in driving up from the lower part of the Notch to the Profile House. Yet the interest of the mountain to visitors has been so concentrated in the Profile, that very few have studied and enjoyed the nobler grandeur on which that countenance is only a fantastic freak. And many, doubtless, have looked up with awe to the Great Stone Face, with a feeling that a grander expression of the Infinite power and art is suggested in it than in any mortal countenance. "Is not this a place," we have heard it said, "to feel the insignificance of man?" Yes, before God, perhaps, but not before matter. The rude volcanic force that puffed the molten rocks into bubbles, has lifted nothing so marvellous in structure as a human skeleton. The earthquakes and the frosts that have shaken and gnawed the granite of Mount Cannon into the rough semblance of an intelligent physiognomy, are not to be compared for wonder to the slow action of the chemistries that groove, chasten, and tint the bones and tissues of a human head into correspondence with the soul that animates it, as it grows in wisdom and moral beauty. The life that veins and girdles the noblest mountain on the earth, is shallow to the play of vital energies within a human frame.

> No mountain can
> Measure with a perfect man.

The round globe itself is only the background upon which the human face in chiselled. Each on of us *wears* more of the Infinite art,—is housed in more of the Infinite beneficence, than is woven into the whole material vesture of New Hampshire. And the mind that can sap the mountain, untwist its structure, and digest the truth it hides,—the taste that enjoys its form and draperies,—the soul whose solemn joy, stirred at first by the spring of its peaks, and the strength of its buttresses, mounts to Him who "toucheth the hills and they smoke,"—these are the voyagers for which the Creator built

> this round sky-cleaving boat
> Which never strains its rocky beams;
> Whose timbers, as they silent float,
> Alps and Caucasus uprear,
> And the long Alleghanies here,
> And all town-sprinkled lands that be,
> Sailing through stars with all their history.

The White Mountain Guide Book, 1863

Samuel C. Eastman

By the middle of the nineteenth century, when visitors were going to the White Mountains in larger and larger numbers, guide books specifically written for these visitors began to appear. Samuel C. Eastman's series of White Mountain guidebooks, first published in 1858, and ultimately in fifteen editions, were some of the most popular such works. Samuel Eastman was born in Concord, New Hampshire, on July 11, 1837. After an education at Brown University and Harvard Law School he returned to Concord and a successful career in law and business. At different times he was a member of the New Hampshire legislature and was once Speaker of the New Hampshire House of Representatives. He was an active member in and President of the New Hampshire Historical Society. His membership on the board of directors of the Profile and Flume Hotel Company is testimony to his interest in Franconia Notch. One biographical sketch reads: "Mr. Eastman is a wide reader, a clear thinker, a logical reasoner, an able lawyer, an erudite scholar, an incisive and effective writer and speaker."

FIRST VIEW OF FRANCONIA

FROM BETHLEHEM there are two roads to Franconia Notch. Whichever we take, we must ascend a high and toilsome hill, but the view from the summit repays us for all our delay. This view, comprehending the whole of the grand Franconia range in front, with the head of Lafayette standing majestically above them all, and on the right the dark opening of the Notch, with long extent of valley and intervale between, is one of the finest views in the day's ride. It remains in sight for some time while you are descending the hill and crossing the valley of the south branch to the Ammonoosuc. Then begins the slow ascent of the Notch. Winding through its shady ravines we come at last to the Profile House.

FRANCONIA NOTCH AND
ITS NEIGHBORHOOD

The Franconia Range of hills, though properly belonging to the White Mountain Range, is still so distinct and peculiar in its character as to deserve a lengthened notice. The beauties of the surrounding scenery entitle it to all the admiration which the tourist bestows upon it. Indeed by old *habitués* of the region, Franconia is considered the gem of the mountains. There is not the overpowering grandeur which belongs to the White Mountains, while the greater variety of interesting objects amply compensates for the absence of more stately scenes. The quiet beauty, and the repose of Nature in the Franconia Notch may well introduce the traveller to the higher sublimity beyond, or refresh him as he retires from the powerful influence which he has felt before the majesty of the North. There is a tranquillity in the former feeling, and a sense of relief in the latter, which prepares or soothes the mind. Here is rest; here is comfort. Beneath the shadow of these solemn mountains, the weary soul finds composure. Selfishness and worldliness are rebuked. The most thoughtless are hushed to reflection and a better understanding of life grows up in the midst of Nature's grand instructions. We do not suppose our tourist is in quest of mere pleasure; we believe him to be a better and nobler man then to spend his days thus. He is open to every good influence, that will make life more rich and beautiful and fair. There is no better influence than that of which he will be sensible, in the still retreat of Franconia...

...But the great marvel and pride of this region is the

PROFILE

As we walk down the road to the south of the hotel, we soon come to a rude bench by the wayside, and, attracted by the guide-board above it, inscribed with the single, simple word, "Profile," as we direct our eyes to the point which it indicates, the huge face with all its features thoroughly delineated, stands out in bold outline, before our sight. There it is, a colossal, completely symmetrical profile, looking down upon the valley from its lofty height, perfectly distinct and clear. The tourist may possibly think that this, like other wonderful stories of which veracious guidebooks tell, may be a myth, and that the similarity may exist only in the fancy of the writer. But no! This time, at least, he will acknowledge, that there is no delusion. Nature has carved out, with the most accurate chiseling, this astonishing sculpture. Every portion of the face is there, upon the solid mountain steep. There is the stern, projecting, massive brow, as though stamped with the thought and wisdom of centuries. The nose is straight, finely cut, and sharply outlined. The thin, senile lips are parted, as though about to utter the thunders of majestic speech. The chin is well thrown forward, with exact proportionate length, betokening the hard, obstinate character of the "Old Man," who has faced, with such unmoving steadiness, the storms of ages. The Sphynx of the Desert must acknowledge its inferiority to this marvelous face upon the mountain. When seen in the morning, as the mists float up from the valley beneath and along its ponderous features, it looms into larger proportions still, and with the heavy gray beard, which sometimes settles upon its chin, and down its breast, it seems like the face of some hoary patriarch of antiquity…

…"It is not advisable," says one of the admirers of the Old Man of the Mountain, "to go to take your first look at him, when the sun lights up the chasm of his granite cheek, and the cavernous mystery of his bent brow. Go to him, when in the solemn light of evening, the mountain heaves up from the darkening lake its vast wave of luxuriant foliage. Sit on one of those rocks by the road-side, and look, if our can, without awe, at the Granite Face, human in its lineaments, supernatural in size and position, weird-like in its shadowy mystery, but its sharp outline wearing an expression of mortal sadness, that gives it the most fascinating interest." …It was doubtless an object of veneration to the aboriginal inhabitants. Various traditionary tales are yet extant respecting the superstitious homage once paid to it by the Indian tribes who frequented the locality. Relics of their life, and singular utensils of a former generation have been found near it. To the whites, however, it has been little known, till within the last forty years. In the early part of the present century, the road that passes along this way was laid out, and in clearing the land of the trees that impeded the path, the profile was discovered. Since that time, it has been an object of the most absorbing interest. The genius of Hawthorne has embalmed it in our literature, and his story of "The Great Stone Face," can only be read appreciatively beneath its shadow...

...The Profile itself undergoes many changes according to the point of observation. It changes from its severe facial outline to a jagged and apparently shapeless mass of rocks, or to a face with a flat forehead, or with a huge, Roman nose, or to the unmeaning, and retreating countenance of some wild animal. It is only at the place where the guide-board is erected, that the Profile is to be most distinctly seen. One can spend an hour or two no more profitably than by gazing upon its fascinating and wonderful lineaments, and he will return to look upon it once more, that it may be the last remembrance, ere he bids farewell to this delightful spot.

Views in the White Mountains with Descriptions

Moses F. Sweetser

The most complete and accurate guidebooks of the nineteenth century were written by Moses F. Sweetser. First published in 1873, Sweetser's guidebooks were printed in a total of fifteen editions, the last being published in 1896, the year before Sweetser's death. These guidebooks contained very detailed information that a White Mountain visitor might use including information about the trails that had been built and the hotel accommodations that were available. In addition to the series of guidebooks, in 1879 Sweetser published *Views of the White Mountains*, an important collection of photographs of the White Mountains. In his travels in the mountains, Sweetser was often accompanied by Joshua H. Huntington, an early pioneer of winter exploration on the summits of the mountains and after whom Huntington Ravine on Mount Washington is named. In both of the below excerpts from Sweetser's writings he refers to "Professor Hitchcock," Charles H. Hitchcock, the New Hampshire State Geologist and a Professor at Dartmouth College.

THE PROFILE, FRANCONIA NOTCH

IN HIS STORY of "The Great Stone Face," Hawthorne speaks of it as "a work of Nature in her mood of majestic playfulness, formed on the perpendicular side of a mountain by some immense rocks, which had been thrown together in such a position, as, when viewed at a proper distance, precisely to resemble the features of the human countenance." Many years later, the brain which conceived the story, and the hand which penned it, were stilled in the slumber of death, within sight of the weird object which he had so well described; and New England was left to mourn.

But there was no playfulness in the heart of Nature when she formed that sad and yearning, that awful and æon-wearied face. It was rather the work and the outward expression of the creation "which groaneth and travaileth,"—a vast and solemn hieroglyph of sorrow, chained like a new Prometheus amid the pealing thunders and the driving snow, and bearing mighty teachings for the true *illuminati*. Who can compare the feminine grace of the Apollo, Belvedere, or the dissecting-room statues of Michael Angelo, with a countenance like this, so grand and desolate, so mysterious and weird?

As we stand by the shore of the lake just south of the Profile House about four o'clock on a summer afternoon, and look upward along the ledgy slopes of Cannon Mountain, the statuesque face is outlined clearly against the bright western sky, with its massive chin, its apparently wavering lips, and its bold projecting brow. Although twelve hundred feet above the lake, and far away on the mountain-side, the lineaments are clear-cut and distinct, for it is forty feet from the forehead to the end of the chin; and if the remainder of the figure could be added, according to Albert Durer's law of human proportions, this Anak of the North would be sixty feet taller than Bunker-Hill Monument.

I have stood, insect-like, upon the brow of the Profile, and perceived that the three great ledges of which it is composed are made up of coarse granite which can be broken off by the hand. They are wasting away every year; and Professor Hitchcock predicts, that, before many decades have passed, the resemblance to the human face will have disappeared. The hapless Indians, who in ancient days performed their simple rites of worship here, have passed away; and Starr King, Thoreau, and Hawthorne may never thread these defiles again, to bring hither their spiritual offerings, with deep and solemn insight. A brighter and more mirthful era has come; and the lake below is covered with gayly-painted boats, the flavors of the Parisian *cuisine* float upward from the Profile House, and the whistle of the railway locomotive echoes through the Notch. Thus the whole face of the scene has changed; and it is surely time for that grim symbol of Melancholia, hung upon the westward cliffs of Franconia, to vanish, and be seen no more forever.

Old Man of the Mountains. Photograph from the author's collection.

The White Mountains Handbook
for Travellers
Twelfth Edition, 1891

Moses F. Sweetser

THE PROFILE

HE PROFILE (formerly called the *Old Man of the Mountain*) is a wonderful semblance of the human face, formed by the ledges on the upper cliffs of Mt. Cannon, finely relieved against the sky and amid picturesque surroundings. It is best seen from a point marked by a guideboard, on the road a short distance S. of the Profile House, and over Profile Lake. The face looks toward the S. E. This is the most remarkable phenomenon of the kind in the world, and has drawn the admiration of myriads of travellers. There is a tradition that it was worshipped by the Indians in ancient time, but this is doubtful. It was discovered in the year 1805, by Francis Whitcomb and Luke Brooks, who were working on the Notch road, and saw it while washing their hands in Profile Lake. They exclaimed, "That is Jefferson," he being then President. It was described in the American Journal of Science in 1828 by Gen. Martin Field, with a grotesque picture attached. Hawthorne's tale of *The Great Stone Face*, and a later book called *Christus Judex*, celebrate this marvellous outline. There is a probability that it may not last for many years longer, on account of the rapid decomposition of the granite, which crumbles under the hand. Prof. Hitchcock says: "I would advise any persons who are anxious to see the Profile for themselves, to hasten to the spot, for fear of disappointment." It is formed of three disconnected ledges of granite, in different vertical lines, their aggregate height being 36-40 ft. (as measured by the State Survey in 1871); and their height above the lake is 1,200 ft. One rock forms the forehead, another the nose and upper lip, and the third the massive chin. Although the expression as seen from the road is melancholy and severe, there are points farther up the ridge where it becomes amiable and pleasant. The best time to make the visit is in the late afternoon when the face is strongly relieved against the bright sky. With the morning light falling upon it, the cheeks appear haggard and sunken.

The Heart of the White Mountains:
Their Legend and Scenery
Samuel Adams Drake

The Heart of the White Mountains: Their Legend and Scenery by Samuel Adams Drake was published in 1882. The book included history, legends and many general descriptions of the White Mountains. *Harper's Magazine* had published Drake's writings in 1881. Drake was born in Boston in 1833 and died in Kennebunkport, Maine, in 1905.

WE ARE STILL advancing in this region of wonders. In our front soars an insuperable mass of forest-shagged rock. Behind it rises the absolutely regal Lafayette. Our footsteps are stayed by the glimmer of water through trees by the road-side. We have reached the summit of the pass.

Six miles of continued ascent from the Flume House have brought us to Profile Lake, which the road skirts. Although a pretty enough piece of water, it is not for itself this lake is resorted to by its thousands, or for being the source of the Pemigewasset, or for its trout—which you take for the reflection of birds on its burnished surface—but for the mountain rising high above, whose wooded slopes it so faithfully mirrors. Now lift the eyes to the bare summit! It is difficult to believe the evidence of the senses! Upon the high cliffs of this mountain is the remarkable and celebrated natural rock sculpture of a human head, which, from a height twelve hundred feet above the lake, has for uncounted ages looked with the same stony stare down the pass upon the windings of the river through its incomparable valley. The profile itself measures about forty feet from the tip of the chin to the flattened crown which imparts to it such a peculiarly antique appearance. All is perfect, except that the forehead is concealed by something like the visor of a helmet. And all this illusion is produced by several projecting crags. It might be said to have been begotten by a thunder-bolt.

Taking a seat within a rustic arbor on the high shore of the lake, one is at liberty to peruse at leisure what, I dare say, is the most extraordinary sight of a lifetime. A change of position varies more or less the character of the expression, which is after all, the marked peculiarity of this monstrous *alto relievo;* for let the spectator turn his gaze vacantly upon the more familiar objects at hand—as he inevitably will, to assure himself that he is not the victim of some strange hallucination—a fascination born neither of admiration nor horror, but strongly partaking of both emotions, draws him irresistibly back to the Dantesque head stuck, like a felon's, on the highest battlements of the pass. The more you may have seen, the more your feelings are disciplined, the greater the confusion of ideas. The moment is come to acknowledge yourself vanquished. This is not merely a face, it is a portrait. This is not the work of some cunning chisel, but a cast from a living head. You feel and will always maintain that those features have had a living and breathing counterpart. Nothing more, nothing less.

But where and what was the original prototype? Not man; since, ages before he was created, the chisel of the Almighty wrought this sculpture upon the rock above us. No, not man; the face is too majestic, too nobly grand, for anything of mortal mould. One of the antique gods may, perhaps, have sat for this archetype of the coming man. And yet not man, we think, for the head will surely hold the same strange converse with futurity when man shall have vanished from the face of the earth.

This gigantic silhouette, which has been dubbed the Old Man of the Mountain, is unquestionably the greatest curiosity of this or any other mountain region. It is unique. But it is not merely curious; nor is it more marvelous for the wonderful accuracy of outline than for the almost superhuman expression of frozen terror it eternally fixes on the vague and shadowy

FRANCONIA NOTCH, FROM THORNTON.

looked as if it had
been raining sunshine;
the road like an endless
grotto of illuminated leaves,
musical with birds, and ex-
haling a thousand perfumes.

Franconia Notch, From Thornton. W. Hamilton Gibson. Included in *The Heart of the White Mountains* by Samuel A.
Drake. New York, 1882. From the author's collection.

distance—a far-away look; an intense and speechless amazement, such as sometimes settles on the faces of the dying at the
moment the soul leaves the body forever—untranslatable into
words, but seeming to declare the presence of some unutter-
able vision, too bright and dazzling for mortal eyes to behold.
The face puts the whole world behind it. It does everything
but speak—nay, you are ready to swear that it is going to speak!
And so this chance jumbling together of a few stones has produced a sculpture before which Art hangs her head.

I renounce in dismay the idea of reproducing the effect on
the reader's mind which this prodigy produced on my own.
Impressions more pronounced, yet at the same time more in-
explicable, have never so effectually overcome that habitual
self-command derived from many experiences of travel among
strange and unaccustomed scenes. From the moment the
startled eye catches it one is aware of a *Presence* which domi-
nates the spirit, first with strange fear, then by that natural revulsion which at such moments makes the imagination
supreme, conducts straight to the supernatural, there to leave
it helplessly struggling in a maze of impotent conjecture. But,
even upon this debatable ground between two worlds, one is
not able to surprise the secret of those lips of marble. The
Sphinx overcomes us by his stony, his disdainful silence. Let
the visitor be ever so unimpassioned, surely he must be more
than mortal to resist the impression of mingled awe, wonder,
and admiration which a first sight of this weird object forces
upon him. He is, indeed less than human if the feeling does not
continually grow and deepen while he looks. The face is so
amazing, that I have often tried to imagine the sensations of
him who first discovered it peering from the top of the mountain with such absorbed, openmouthed wonder. Again I see
the tired Indian hunter, pausing to slake his thirst by the lakeside, start as his gaze suddenly encounters this terrific appari-
tion. I fancy the half-uttered exclamation sticking in his throat.
I behold him standing there with bated breath, not daring to
stir hand or foot, his white lips parted, his scared eyes dilated,
until his own swarthy features exactly reflect that unearthly,

Eagle Cliff and the Echo House. W. Hamilton Gibson. Included in *The Heart of the White Mountains* by Samuel A. Drake. New York, 1882. From the author's collection.

that intense amazement stamped large and vivid upon the livid rock. There he remains, rooted to the spot, unable to reason, trembling in every limb. For him there are no accidents of nature; for him everything has its design. His moment of terrible suspense is hardly difficult to understand, seeing how careless thousands that come and go are thrilled, and awed, and silenced, notwithstanding you tell them the face is nothing but rocks.

If the effect upon minds of the common order be so pronounced, a first sight of the Great Stone Face may easily be supposed to act powerfully upon the imaginative and impressible. The novelist, Hawthorne, makes it the interpreter of a noble life. For him the Titanic countenance is radiant with majestic benignity. He endows it with a soul, surrounds the colossal brow with the halo of a spiritual grandeur, and, marshalling his train of phantoms, proceeds to pass inexorable judgment upon them... .

Had Byron visited this place of awe and mystery, his "Manfred," the scene of which is laid among the mountains of the Bernese Alps, would doubtless have had a deeper and perhaps gloomier impulse; but even among the eternal realms of ice the poet never beheld an object that could so arouse the gloomy exaltation he has breathed into that tragedy. His line—"Bound to earth, he lifts his eye to heaven"—becomes descriptive here.

Again and again we turn to the face. We go away to wonder if it is still there. We come back to wonder still more. An emotion of pity mingles with the rest. Time seems to have passed it by. It seems undergoing some terrible sentence. It is a greater riddle than the gigantic stone face on the banks of the Nile.

All effects of light and shadow are so many changes of countenance or of expression. I have seen the face cut sharp and clear as an antique cameo upon the morning sky. I have seen it suffused, nay, almost transfigured, in the sunset glow. Often and often does a cloud rest upon its brow. I have seen it start fitfully out of the flying scud to be the next moment smothered in clouds. I have heard the thunder roll from its lips of stone. I recall the sunken cheeks, wet with the damps of its night-long vigil, glistening in the morning sunshine—smiling through tears. I remember its emaciated visage streaked and crossed with wrinkles that the snow had put there in a night; but never have I seen it insipid or commonplace. On the contrary, the overhanging brow, the antique nose, the protruding under-lip, the massive chin, might belong to another Prometheus chained to the rock, but whom no punishment could make lower his haughty head.

I lingered by the margin of the lake watching the play of the clouds upon the water, until a loud and resonant peal, followed by large, warm drops, admonished me to seek the nearest shelter. And what thunder! The hills rocked. What echoes! The mountains seemed knocking their stony heads together. What lightning! The very heavens cracked with the flashes.

> "Far along
> From peak to peak the rattling crags among
> Leaps the live thunder! not from one lone cloud,
> But every mountain now hath found a tongue,
> And Jura answers, through her misty shroud,
> Back to the joyous Alps, who call to her aloud!"

Greetings from the White Mountains. Postcard published by Chisholm Bros., Portland Me. From the author's collection.

PROFILE HOUSE

Franconia Notch, White Mountains, N.H.

(The largest Hotel in New England.)

TAFT & GREENLEAF, Proprietors.

C. H. GREENLEAF, of The Vendome, Boston.

Open from June 20th to October 1st.

POST-OFFICE ADDRESS: PROFILE HOUSE, N.H

How to Reach the Profile House.—ALL Rail, and through in one day from Boston, Newport, New York, Saratoga, Lake George, Montreal, Quebec, Portland, etc., via Profile and Franconia Notch R.R. from Bethlehem Junction: or by DAILY STAGES, via Flume House to Pemigewasset Valley R.R.,—10 miles,—connecting with trains to and from Boston, New York, and all points.

EXCURSIONS.

OBSERVATION WAGONS THROUGH THE NOTCH TWICE DAILY,

FOR

OLD MAN OF THE MOUNTAIN,

FLUME, POOL, BASIN,

AND ALL POINTS OF INTEREST.

Guests, by taking the morning train on the Profile and Franconia Notch Railroad, can visit the Summit of MT. WASHINGTON, or go through the WHITE MOUNTAIN NOTCH to NORTH CONWAY, or visit JEFFERSON or BETHLEHEM, and returning, reach Profile House by rail same day.

Good Bridle and Foot-Paths to the summit of Lafayette, Cannon and Bald Mountains: also, pleasant walks to the Cascade and Echo and Profile Lakes. Upon Echo Lake a small steamer, and upon both Lakes safe row-boats can be had.

The Stables are supplied with the best of Livery and Saddle Horses.

Advertisement for the Profile House, Franconia Notch, *Chisholm's White Mountain Guide, 1880.* From the author's collection.

THE PROFILE HOUSE

Chisholm's White Mountain Guide Book
Hugh J. Chisholm

Hugh J. Chisholm recognized the growing tourist industry in the White Mountains. In 1880 he published the first of many guide books to the region.

HE PROFILE HOUSE, in a narrow glen near the head of the famous pass, is the capital of all this region, and gives shelter to 500 guests at once, with all the soft luxuries of our patrician age, the *bric-a-brac* shop, post and telegraph offices, billiard and bowling rooms, a barber shop, gas-lights, a dining room fit for a conclave of cardinals, connected villas, and a busy livery-stable. The cliff-enwalled basis on which this wilderness-palace stands is 1,974 feet above the sea.

In 1879 a narrow-gauge railroad was built from the standard tracks at Bethlehem Junction, running through nearly ten miles of forests, and finding its terminus near the Profile House, from which, however, it is happily concealed by a screen of groves. By this route, the Franconia Notch is made very accessible to the outer world, while its manifold beauties have been judiciously saved from blemish. To the southward, the stages still roll away down the Notch to the terminus of the new Pemigewasset Valley Railroad, ten miles from the Profile and five miles from the Flume. The Profile House is and must remain the great centre for all excursions in this lovely Franconian region, whose manifold and diversified attractions are so worthy of observation.

The White Mountains: A Handbook for Travellers, 1891

Moses F. Sweetser

THE PROFILE HOUSE is one of the best summer-hotels in the United States. It accommodates 5-600 guests, at $4.50 a day, with reductions for permanent boarders. Its dining-hall is the finest in the mountain-region; and in point of cuisine it compares favorably with the Glen House. The parlor is 100x50 feet in area, and is the scene of brilliant evening assemblies. There are post and telegraph offices, billiard-halls and bowling-alleys, bath-rooms, a barber-shop, a salesroom for pictures and knick-knacks, a livery-stable, passenger elevator, and four tennis-courts. Band and orchestra concerts daily in the hall, and on Profile Lake. S. of the hotel are five villas, leased by the season. The house is surrounded with verandas; and its environs are kept with rare neatness. This is a favorite resort for New Yorkers, Bostonians and Philadelphians.

THE PROFILE HOUSE.

The Profile House. Moses F. Sweetser. *Views of the White Mountains,* Boston, 1879. From the author's collection.

Profile House, Franconia Notch, August 12, 1873: An Avalanche Of Visitors

Excerpts from an unknown newspaper*

T IS THE HEIGHT of the season in this wonderful city of the Notch, the apex of excitement, fashion, travel, shut in between these grand Franconia Mountains. For a week, now, the world in its finest feathers has flown hither, and crammed every nook and corner of this immense house, where the cream of society never fails to rise sooner or later. Last Friday night, four hundred and ninety guests slept under the shadow of the Profile, and then "the height" was pronounced as reached. Slept, did I say? Well, some did and some didn't. One can't sleep in the hair-dressers chair, or any other chair, much. And many of this travelling army were forced to double up, sometimes six deep, in a room, and stretched their wearied limbs on cots or mattresses, just for the sake of being where everybody else wished to be, and would be in spite of warnings to the contrary. Including the employes, there were over seven hundred mouths to be fed. To say nothing of the lodgings to be provided, this responsibility seems enough to turn one's hair white. Fancy the larders, and fancy if there shouldn't have been enough supplies to go round! Saturday night it was even more crowded, and when the last stages came in, the entrance and corridors were thronged with as brilliant a multitude as could be found in Fifth avenue. The more fortunate spectators, who were well provided with rooms, gave a murmur that, if I had been one of the late comers, I shouldn't have relished. It was decidedly derisive, a what-is-going-to-become-of-you tone, that the unconscious travelers didn't comprehend, or they would have sat on the piazza and wept. It

---

*Reprinted courtesy of the Dartmouth College Library.

was so immensely funny, people seemed to think, that the house couldn't hold another solitary being, and every man and woman were destined to cots or an onward ride to the "Flume." The proprietors had telegraphed over forty not to come—there was no room; but such is the force of determination, or that hope springing eternal in the human breast, on they came and trusted to luck. Six ladies occupied one room that ordinarily holds two, and their respective husbands had mattresses in a reception room. Men's fate under a pressure of travel is of the hardiest; anything will do for them. Besides the stageloads, parties had been driving up all day, only to be sent away to the great resource, the Flume House; but when it grew dusk, and yet another wagon load appeared, nothing was to be done but give them shelter and stand-up beds, as I heard a lady say.

COLD

The mornings and evenings have been so cold that great wood fires burnt in the little parlor and hall. So cheery as they are, giving a homelike air to the house, and something for people to gather about! A dozen ladies or more were sitting around the hall fire, this morning, chatting with the gentlemen who smoked the after-breakfast cigar. Groups of shawled and parasoled damsels sat out in the sunshine; others, freshly caparisoned in white toilets, ventured to walk up and down the piazza; a flood of sunlight filled the grounds and threw deep shadows up the mountain side. The air is as crisp as October, full of exhilaration, and that peculiar quality that draws out all one's dilapidated nerves, replacing them with an elation sufficient to walk one up Mount Lafayette.

NEW YORKERS

The Profile is essentially a New York house, and just at present about two hundred guests are from that city. They really fill the house, and give it the reputation for style and elegance for which it is distinguished. There is always a struggle for rooms, and all the families who are here summer after summer engage a year ahead. Wm. H. Vanderbilt's family occupy fourteen rooms, and once a week the millionaire takes his palace car and spends Sunday in delicious coolness at the Profile.

SUNDAY

Last Sunday the drawing-room was filled with a very large audience to hear Mr. Bancroft, of Brooklyn, read the service and preach. I have never seen a more circumspect and attentive congregation in church. With very few exceptions, the whole house attended. The singing was by some young ladies from Brooklyn and New York. It is a wonder the whole crowd were not made ill by the dampness of the place. Windows were open and blinds shut, and it was cold enough out of doors to freeze one, except right in the sun. Yet vain and lovely beings came to confess their sins in their white dresses garnished with lace and dainty ribbons through which could be seen their round arms and pretty shoulders! A very stylish young girl sat in front of me, with only one thickness of cambric over her neck; but then she had a jet collar holding up her Elizabethan ruff and that might have kept her warm. It was a great relief to see Dr. Peters of New York, the other side of her, in case she had an attack of pneumonia, before service was over.

A Newspaper Article
Date and Paper, Unknown

HE PROFILE HOUSE, Franconia, is widely known and popular House, located in a beautiful and picturesque section. The house is built upon a level spot of ground, surrounded by Eagle Cliff on the left and Mount Cannon on the right. Contiguous to the house is Echo and Profile Lakes at which points the Old Man of the Mountain is distinctly seen. The house is capable of accommodating 425 guests, number of help employed 125. At the head of its management stands Mr. and Mrs. Taft, than whom, no better can be found. Associated with these pioneers in hotel keeping, is Mr. and Mrs. Greenleaf, both of whom are well qualified to fill their respective positions: The proprietors are men of large business capacity and conduct their house in a good and orderly manner. Their gentlemanly and efficient clerk, Isaac Andrews, comes in for a special notice; he is prompt, urbane and attentive to the wants of guests. The cost of this magnificent house, as stated by the proprietors, was $160,000. In connection with the house is a good billiard and bowling hall for those who enjoy such recreations, also a livery stable, containing 35 fine horses for use of patrons. In short, this is the most popular of all the mountain houses. About half a mile down the road, is one of the greatest curiosities to be found in all the region of the White Mountains, to wit, a fish house for propagating the beautiful spotted trout, for which the arrangements are perfect, and there are to be seen some 10,000 fish, from four months to four years old; of the latter there are some 1,500, the most inviting fish department ever witnessed by the writer. At the time of writing the house contained some two hundred guests. Among those was the far-famed Commodore W. H. Vanderbilt, and suit, of New York. Mr. Vanderbilt is a gentleman of marked

Echo Lake and the Profile House. Illustration from a 19th Century souvenir Book. From the author's collection.

characteristics, plain to be seen by an observing eye. The next guest of note to be named are Mr. W. J. Smith and daughter. This gentlemen is upwards of three-score years of age, he is a hale, jovial and pleasant man and carries in his open and frank countenance, the evidence of heart, soul and magnanimity, the same can be said of his accomplished and interesting daughter. More might be said, but at this time deponent saith not— time and space bids him stop.

A Trip to The White Mountains
Harper's Weekly, August 22, 1857

MY NAME IS Peter Plum.* You will not find it in this year's Directory. When I withdrew from business I took it out, intending to go and live in Europe for a couple of years. Circumstances which are no business of yours have detained me here. Mayn't I do as I please?

When Mrs. P. said to me, "My dear, we would like to go to the White Mountains this August," I knew how it would be. I knew that we should be horridly bored, and worried to death with all manner of inconveniences; that a month on Blackwell's Island, or a short term in the Penitentiary would be preferable in many respects; but as my old father used to say, "Peter, when your wife says, 'We would like,' that means, 'My boy, you must:'" so I answered, "Mrs. P., when will you leave?"

…Of course you don't want me to describe the agony of the trip from our landing-place to Boston and Portland. I can only account for the elaborate discomfort of the journey on the supposition that the New Englanders desire to discourage travel in their direction. Our party were separated in the cars. I shared a seat with a stout young woman, who I suspect was a wet-nurse by trade; she rather startled me by telling me to "lean on her," if I wanted: as I hastily disavowed any intention of such a proceeding, she said "it was all one, she would lean on me;" and so she did, as I'm a sinner! the whole livelong night. She left a hair-pin in my vest, which led to the first quarrel I have ever had with my Betsey.

By hook and crook we made our way from Boston to Portland, from Portland to Franconia. We put up at a hotel there, and I expected a respite from our miseries. I ordered a private

---

Editor's Note: The author of this piece refers to a number of people including: Alice, his daughter; Harrison Van Buren, his son; Short, the daughter's friend and therefore the author's prospective son-in-law; And lastly, Betsey, the author's wife.

The Old Man of the Mountain. Illustration in *Harper's Weekly,*
August 22, 1857.

dinner of lamb-chops, with some claret I had brought with me, and started out with our party to see a hideous rock, which they call the Old Man of the Mountain—and which, between you and me, is like anything you wish to fancy. It was hard work getting to the right place to see the Old Man; and our guide enlivened the journey by telling us that here a party of travelers had been eaten by bears, there a hunter had fallen over the rocks, and there a pair of horses had been crushed by a landslide; but at last we got there, and sat down, without bears or landslides. Well, I was comfortable once more, when that silly girl Alice drags us to a narrow ledge to watch some absurd artist who was sketching the Old Man. The artist (I must do him the justice to say he was a mild-spoken person) observed that the rock was not strong enough to bear so many; but Betsey would have me see the rock in the best light, and so I went, and we all went, and, as might have been expected, while we were gazing with open mouths, the ledge gave way, and down we all went into a pool beneath. We escaped with nothing worse than a ducking; but Harrison Van Buren came down on his mother's nose, and somewhat injured that feature.

Returning to the hotel, we found our lamb-chops in a state of cinder, and the claret uncorked—to save time, the waiter said. I bore all, however, feeling that it was in the order of things, and fulfilled my destiny by pursuing our journey to the Crawford House.

...No sir; the White Mountains are very well no doubt, for young lovers and romantic fools (my daughter and Short protest they enjoyed themselves prodigiously, and never visited so delightful a place); but when next you hear of Peter Plum making an ass of himself by journeying to that or any other fashionable place of summer resort—when you hear of him leaving his comfortable house in the Avenue to follow the multitude into such follies, and making himself miserable under the name of enjoyment,—when you hear of this, Sir, again, why just call on him, and demand his check for a thousand dollars. It will be paid.

The White Mountain Series:
The Profile House
Boston 1872—A fictional account
Percy Curtiss

HERE IS PROBABLY no house in the United States, where one is more agreeably disappointed after its first reception, that at the Profile House. To alight from the top of the stage-coach, after several hours' ride, during which we have experienced great physical and intellectual tension, and to find similar stage-loads of human beings constantly arriving from all parts of the country, is not conducive to rest or sweetness of temper. The piazzas are full of people—people to be envied for they know where they are to sleep, and have their delightful excursions or equally delightful repose, mapped out for the morrow. The halls and stairways are filled with strangers who are waiting for rooms, and they are all as much alike as dust and hunger can make them.

The clerk from his stand at the office, looks helplessly at this surging mass of humanity, well knowing that he cannot supply one room where six will be demanded, although the hotel is large, and offers the very best and most comfortable accommodations.

As soon as Ralph had assisted his mother to the reception room, he took his place in the line of new-comers which terminated opposite the clerk. Before he had reached that goal, he understood the situation—learned that so many telegrams were received from all quarters, that no attention could be paid to any—and thankfully accepted three rooms, in the place of the six he had ordered. This was understood to be a temporary arrangement, until the clerk could "see what could be done."

After this settlement had been effected, Ralph found Gustavus Freelingheit leaning against one of the wooden pil-

Echo Lake, Franconia Notch. Moses F. Sweetser. *Views of the White Mountains,* Boston, 1879. From the author's collection

lars, looking with an air of disgust at the rapidly dispersing crowd before him.

"What are you doing, Gus?"

"Waiting till the clerk 'sees what can be done about a room'."

"Then you'll wait all night," replied Ralph, who had become convinced that "seeing what could be done" was a dilemma that was nothing but horns: that in their present situation fascination and forlornness were at equal discount, that common and uncommon sense were equally valueless, and that if by any chance one could get a foothold in the house, it should be accepted and retained.

...It would probably be a difficult matter to build a hotel large enough to accommodate the immense crowds who flock to this locality during the heated term of the summer.

The Profile House is excelled by no hotel in the State. It contains a parlor nearly one hundred by fifty feet, with fine rooms in the second and third stories. It is situated in the immediate vicinity of Echo Lake, Cannon Mountain, Eagle Cliff, The Profile, and Mount Lafayette. It is on a level plain, a few acres in area, in the bosom of the hills. It has two approaches; on the north from Bethlehem and Littleton—on the south, from the Flume House and the Pemigewasset Valley. All around the house, the mountains stand in most august proportions, when relieved by the dark blue of a clear summer's day. The location of the hotel, the clear bracing air of the Notch, and the pure water of the hills, combine in giving one an excellent appetite and good digestion. In this favored spot, the traveller finds clean rooms, faithful attention, a profuse table, and beauty of locality.

The Great Stone Face

Nathaniel Hawthorne

THE GREAT STONE FACE

The Great Stone Face
Nathaniel Hawthorne

Nathaniel Hawthorne's legend of *The Great Stone Face* has long been one of the most popular stories about the Profile. Hawthorne started this story in 1840 and completed it eight years later. Hawthorne received $25 when the story was published in January 1850 in *The National Era*, a magazine edited by John Greenleaf Whittier.

Nathaniel Hawthorne was born on July 4, 1804 in Salem, Massachusetts. His father was a sea captain who died of yellow fever in Dutch Guiana (now Surinam) when Hawthorne was very young. He spent much of his youth in Maine and graduated from Bowdoin College in 1825. After that Hawthorne returned to Salem to have a career as a professional writer. He first visited the White Mountains and Franconia Notch in 1832 where he was a guest of Ethan Allen Crawford. During the Presidential campaign of 1852 he wrote a campaign biography, *Life of Franklin Pierce,* for his college friend. Hawthorne and Pierce maintained their friendship throughout and after Pierce's single term in office. On May 19, 1864, while he was accompanying Pierce on a visit to Plymouth, New Hampshire, Hawthorne died in his sleep, a short forty miles from Franconia Notch and "The Great Stone Face."

The Great Stone Face

ONE AFTERNOON, when the sun was going down, a mother and her little boy sat at the door of their cottage, talking about the Great Stone Face. They had but to lift their eyes, and there it was plainly to be seen, though miles away, with the sunshine brightening all its features.

And what was the Great Stone Face?

Embosomed amongst a family of lofty mountains, there was a valley so spacious that it contained many thousand inhabitants. Some of these good people dwelt in log-huts, with the black forest all around them, on the steep and difficult hillsides. Others had their homes in comfortable farm-houses, and cultivated the rich soil on the gentle slopes or level surfaces of the valley. Others, again, were congregated into populous villages, where some wild, highland rivulet, tumbling down from its birthplace in the upper mountain region, had been caught and tamed by human cunning, and compelled to turn the machinery of cotton factories The inhabitants of this valley, in short, were numerous, and of many modes of life. But all of them, grown people and children, had a kind of familiarity with the Great Stone Face, although some possessed the gift of distinguishing this grand natural phenomenon more perfectly than many of their neighbors.

The Great Stone Face, then, was a work of Nature in her mood of majestic playfulness, formed on the perpendicular side of a mountain by some immense rocks, which had been thrown together in such a position as, when viewed at a proper distance, precisely to resemble the features of the human countenance. It seemed as if an enormous giant, or a Titan, had sculptured his own likeness on the precipice. There was the broad arch of the forehead, a hundred feet in height; the nose, with its long bridge; and the vast lips, which, if they could have spoken, would have rolled their thunder accents from one end of the valley to the other. True it is, that if the spectator approached too near, he lost the outline of the gigantic visage, and could discern only a heap of ponderous and gigantic rocks, piled in chaotic ruin one upon another. Retracing his steps, however, the wondrous features would again be seen; and the farther he withdrew from them, the more like a human face, with all its original divinity intact, did they appear; until, as it grew dim in the distance, with the clouds and glorified vapor of the mountains clustering about it, the Great Stone Face seemed positively to be alive.

It was a happy lot for children to grow up to manhood or womanhood with the Great Stone Face before their eyes, for all the features were noble, and the expression was at once grand and sweet, as if it were the glow of a vast, warm heart, that embraced all mankind in its affections, and had room for more. It was an education only to look at it. According to the belief of many people, the valley owed much of its fertility to this benign aspect that was continually beaming over it, illuminating the clouds, and infusing its tenderness into the sunshine.

As we began with saying, a mother and her little boy sat at their cottage-door, gazing at the Great Stone Face, and talking about it. The child's name was Ernest.

"Mother," said he, while the Titanic visage smiled on him, "I wish that it could speak, for it looks so very kindly that its voice must needs be pleasant. If I were to see a man with such a face, I should love him dearly."

"If an old prophecy should come to pass," answered his mother, "we may see a man, some time or other, with exactly such a face as that."

"What prophecy do you mean, dear mother?" eagerly inquired Ernest. "Pray tell me all about it!"

So his mother told him a story that her own mother had told to her, when she herself was younger than little Ernest; a story, not of things that were past, but of what was yet to come; a story, nevertheless, so very old, that even the Indians, who formerly inhabited this valley, had heard it from their forefathers, to whom, as they affirmed, it had been murmured by the mountain streams, and whispered by the wind among the tree-tops. The purport was, that, at some future day, a child should be born hereabouts, who was destined to become the greatest and noblest personage of his time, and whose countenance, in manhood, should bear an exact resemblance to the Great Stone Face. Not a few old-fashioned people, and young ones likewise, in the ardor of their hopes, still cherished an enduring faith in this old prophecy. But others, who had seen more of the world, had watched and waited till they were weary, and had beheld no man with such a face, nor any man that proved to be much greater or nobler than his neighbors, concluded it to be nothing but an idle tale. At all events, the great man of the prophecy had not yet appeared.

"O mother, dear mother!" cried Ernest, clapping his hands above his head, "I do hope that I shall live to see him!"

His mother was an affectionate and thoughtful woman, and felt that it was wisest not to discourage the generous hopes of her little boy. So she only said to him, "Perhaps you may."

And Ernest never forgot the story that his mother told him. It was always in his mind, whenever looked upon the Great Stone Face. He spent his childhood in the log-cottage where he was born, and was dutiful to his mother, and helpful to her in many things, assisting her much with his little hands, and more with his loving heart. In this manner, from a happy yet often pensive child, he grew up to be a mild, quiet, unobtrusive boy, and sun-browned with labor in the fields, but with more intelligence brightening his aspect than is seen in many lads who have been taught at famous schools. Yet Ernest had had no teacher, save only that the Great Stone Face became one to him. When the toil of the day was over, he would gaze at it for hours, until he began to imagine that those vast features recognized him, and gave him a smile of kindness and encouragement, responsive to his own look of veneration. We must not take upon us to affirm that this was a mistake, although the Face may have looked no more kindly at Ernest than at all the world besides. But the secret was that the boy's

The Great Stone Face. Postcard published by Chisholm Bros., Portland, Me. From the author's collection.

tender and confiding simplicity discerned what other people could not see; and thus the love, which was meant for all, became his peculiar portion.

About this time there went a rumor throughout the valley, that the great man, foretold from ages long ago, who was to bear a resemblance to the Great Stone face, had appeared at last. It seems that, many years before, a young man had migrated from the valley and settled at a distant seaport, where, after getting together a little money, he had set up as a shop-keeper. His name—but I could never learn whether it was his real one, or a nickname that had grown out of his habits and success in life—was Gathergold. Being shrewd and active, and endowed by Providence with that inscrutable faculty which develops itself in what the world calls luck, he became an exceedingly rich merchant, and owner of a whole fleet of bulky-bottomed ships. All the countries of the globe appeared to join hands for the mere purpose of adding heap after heap to the mountainous accumulation of this one man's wealth. The cold regions of the north, almost within the gloom and shadow of the Arctic Circle, sent him their tribute in the shape of furs; hot Africa sifted for him the golden sands of her rivers, and gathered up the ivory tusks of her great elephants out of the forests; the East came bringing him the rich shawls, and spices, and teas, and the effulgence of diamonds, and the gleaming purity of large pearls. The ocean, not to be behindhand with the earth, yielded up her mighty whales, that Mr. Gathergold might sell their oil, and make a profit on it. Be the original commodity what it might, it was gold within his grasp. It might be said of him, as of Midas, in the fable, that whatever he touched with his finger immediately glistened, and grew yellow, and was changed at once into sterling metal, or, which suited him still better, into piles of coin. And, when Mr. Gathergold had become so very rich that it would have taken him a hundred years only to count his wealth, he bethought himself of his native valley, and resolved to go back thither, and end his days where he was born. With this purpose in view, he sent a skilful architect to build him such a palace as should be fit for a man of his vast wealth to live in. As I have said above, it had already been rumored in the valley that Mr. Gathergold had turned out to be the prophetic personage so long and vainly looked for, and that his visage was the perfect and undeniable similitude of the Great Stone Face. People were the more ready to believe that this must needs be the fact when they beheld the splendid edifice that rose, as by enchantment, on the site of his father's old weather beaten farm-house. The exterior was of marble, dazzlingly white that it seemed as though the whole structure might melt away in the sunshine, like those humbler ones which Mr. Gathergold, in his young play-days, before his fingers were gifted with the touch of transmutation, had been accustomed to build of snow. It had a richly ornamented portico, supported by tall pillars, beneath which was a lofty door, studded with silver knobs, and made of a kind of variegated wood that had been brought from beyond the sea. The windows, from the floor to the ceiling of each stately apartment, were composed, respectively, of but one enormous pane of glass, so transparently pure that it was said to be a finer medium than even the vacant atmosphere. Hardly anybody had been permitted to see the interior of this palace; but it was reported, and with good semblance of truth, to be far more gorgeous than the outside, insomuch that, whatever was iron or brass in other houses was silver or gold in this; and Mr. Gathergold's bedchamber, especially made such a glittering appearance that no ordinary man would have been able to close his eyes there. But, on the other hand, Mr. Gathergold was now so inured to wealth, that perhaps he could not have closed his eyes, unless where the gleam of it was certain to find its way beneath his eyelids.

In due time, the mansion was finished; next came the upholsterers, with magnificent furniture; then, a whole troop of black and white servants, the harbingers of Mr. Gathergold, who, in his own majestic person, was expected to arrive at sunset. Our friend Ernest, meanwhile, had been deeply stirred by the idea that the great man, the noble man, the man of prophecy, after so many ages of delay, was at length to be made manifest to his native valley. He knew, boy as he was, that there were a thousand ways in which Mr. Gathergold, with his vast wealth, might transform himself into an angel of beneficence, and assume a control over human affairs as wide and benignant as the smile of the Great Stone Face. Full of faith and hope, Ernest doubted not that what the people said was true, and that now he was to behold the living likeness of those wondrous features on the mountain-side. While the boy was still gazing up the valley, and fancying, as he always did, that the Great Stone Face returned his gaze and looked kindly at him, the rumbling of wheels was heard, approaching swiftly along the winding road.

"Here he comes!" cried a group of people who were assembled to witness the arrival. "Here comes the great Mr. Gathergold!"

A carriage, drawn by four horses, dashed round the turn of the road. Within it, thrust partly out of the window, appeared the physiognomy of the old man, with a skin as yellow as if his own Midas hand had transmuted it. He had a low forehead, small, sharp eyes, puckered about with innumerable wrinkles, and very thin lips, which he made still thinner by pressing them forcibly together.

"The very image of the Great Stone Face!" shouted the people. "Sure enough, the old prophecy is true; and here we have the great man come, at last!"

And, what greatly perplexed Ernest, they seemed actually to believe that here was the likeness which they spoke of. By the roadside there chanced to be an old beggar-woman and two little beggar-children, stragglers from some far-off region, who, as the carriage rolled onward, held out their hands and lifted up their doleful voices, most piteously beseeching charity. A yellow claw—the very same that had clawed together so much wealth—poked itself out of the coach-window, and dropt some copper coins upon the ground; so that, though the great

man's name seems to have been Gathergold, he might just as suitably have been nicknamed Scattercopper. Still, nevertheless, with an earnest shout, and evidently with as much good faith as ever, the people bellowed,—
"He is the very image of the Great Stone Face!"
But Ernest turned sadly from the wrinkled shrewdness of that sordid visage, and gazed up the valley, where, amid a gathering mist, gilded by the last sunbeams, he could still distinguish those glorious features which had impressed themselves into his soul. Their aspect cheered him. What did the benign lips seem to say?
"He will come! Fear not, Ernest; the man will come!"

The years went on, and Ernest ceased to be a boy. He had grown to be a young man now. He attracted little notice from the other inhabitants of the valley; for they saw nothing remarkable in his way of life, save that, when the labor of the day was over, he still loved to go apart and gaze and meditate upon the Great Stone Face. According to their idea of the matter, it was a folly, indeed, but pardonable, inasmuch as Ernest was industrious, kind, and neighborly, and neglected no duty for the sake of indulging this idle habit. They knew not that the Great Stone Face had become a teacher to him, and that the sentiment which was expressed in it would enlarge the young man's heart, and fill it with wider and deeper sympathies than other hearts. They knew not that thence would come a better wisdom than could be learned from books, and a better life than could be moulded on the defaced example of other human lives. Neither did Ernest know that the thoughts and affections which came to him so naturally, in the fields and at the fireside, and wherever he communed with himself, were of a higher tone than those which all men shared with him. A simple soul,—simple as when his mother first taught him the old prophecy,—he beheld the marvellous features beaming adown the valley, and still wondered that their human counterpart was so long in making his appearance.

By this time poor Mr. Gathergold was dead and buried; and the oddest part of the matter was, that his wealth, which was the body and spirit of his existence, had disappeared before his death, leaving nothing of him but a living skeleton, covered over with a wrinkled, yellow skin. Since the melting away of his gold, it had been very generally conceded that there was no such striking resemblance, after all, betwixt the ignoble features of the ruined merchant and that majestic face upon the mountain-side. So the people ceased to honor him during his lifetime, and quietly consigned him to forgetfulness after his decease. Once in a while, it is true, his memory was brought up in connection with the magnificent palace which he had built, and which had long ago been turned into a hotel for the accommodation of strangers, multitudes of whom came, every summer, to visit that famous natural curiosity, the Great Stone Face. Thus, Mr. Gathergold being discredited and thrown into the shade, the man of prophecy was yet to come.

It so happened that a native-born son of the valley, many years before, had enlisted as a soldier, and, after a great deal of hard fighting, had now become an illustrious commander. Whatever he may be called in history, he was known in camps and on the battle-field, under the nickname of Old Blood-and-Thunder. This war-worn veteran, being now infirm with age and wounds, and weary of the turmoil of military life, and of the roll of the drum and the clangor of the trumpet, that had so long been ringing in his ears, had lately signified a purpose of returning to his native valley, hoping to find repose where he remembered to have left it. The inhabitants, his neighbors and their grown-up children, were resolved to welcome the renowned warrior with a salute of cannon and a public dinner; and all the more enthusiastically, it being affirmed that now, at last, the likeness of the Great Stone Face had actually appeared. An aid-de-camp of Old Blood-and-Thunder, travelling through the valley, was said to have been struck with the resemblance. Moreover, the schoolmates and early acquaintances of the general were ready to testify, on oath, that, to the best of their recollection, the aforesaid general had been exceedingly like the majestic image, even when a boy, only that the idea had never occurred to them at that period. Great, therefore, was the excitement throughout the valley; and many people, who had never once thought of glancing at the Great Stone Face for years before, now spent their time in gazing at it, for the sake of knowing exactly how General Blood-and-Thunder looked.

On the day of the great festival, Ernest, with all the other people of the valley, left their work, and proceeded to the spot where the sylvan banquet was prepared. As he approached, the loud voice of the Rev. Dr. Battleblast was heard, beseeching a blessing on the good things set before them, and on the distinguished friend of peace in whose honor they were assembled. The tables were arranged in a cleared space of the woods, shut in by the surrounding trees, except where a vista opened eastward, and afforded a distant view of the Great Stone Face. Over the general's chair, which was a relic from the home of Washington, there was an arch of verdant boughs, with the laurel profusely intermixed, and surmounted by his country's banner, beneath which he had won his victories. Our friend Ernest raised himself on his tiptoes, in hopes to get a glimpse of the celebrated guest; but there was a mighty crowd about the tables anxious to hear the toasts and speeches, and to catch any word that might fall from the general in reply; and a volunteer company, doing duty as a guard, pricked ruthlessly with their bayonets at any particularly quiet person among the throng. So Ernest, being of an unobtrusive character, was thrust quite into the background, where he could see no more of Old Blood-and-Thunder's physiognomy than if it had been still blazing on the battle-field. To console himself, he turned towards the Great Stone Face, which, like a faithful and long-remembered friend, looked back and smiled upon him trough the vista of the forest. Meantime, however, he could overhear the remarks of various individuals, who were comparing the features the hero with the face on the distant mountain-side.

" 'T is the same face, to a hair!" cried one man, cutting a caper for joy.

"Wonderfully like, that's a fact!" responded another.

"Like! why, I call it Old Blood-and-Thunder himself, in a monstrous looking-glass!" cried a third.

"And why not? He's the greatest man of this or any other age, beyond a doubt." And then all three of the speakers gave a great shout, which communicated electricity to the crowd, and called forth a roar from a thousand voices, that went reverberating for miles among the mountains, until you might have supposed that the Great Stone Face had poured its thunder-breath into the cry. All these comments, and this vast enthusiasm, served the more to interest our friend; nor did he think of questioning that now, at length, the mountain-visage had found its human counterpart. It is true, Ernest had imagined that this long-looked-for personage would appear in the character of a man of peace, uttering wisdom, and doing good, and making people happy. But, taking an habitual breadth of view, with all his simplicity, he contended that Providence should choose its own method of blessing mankind, and could conceive that this great end might be effected even by a warrior and a bloody sword, should inscrutable wisdom see fit to order matters so.

"The general! the general" was now the cry. "Hush! silence! Old Blood and-Thunder's going to make a speech."

Even so; for, the cloth being removed, the general's health had been drunk, amid shouts of applause, and he now stood upon his feet to thank the company. Ernest saw him. There he was, over the shoulders of the crowd, from the two glittering epaulets and embroidered collar upward, beneath the arch of green boughs with intertwined laurel, and the banner drooping as if to shade his brow! And there, too, visible in the same glance, through the vista of the forest, appeared the Great Stone Face! And was there, indeed, such a resemblance as the crowd had testified? Alas, Ernest could not recognize it! He beheld a war-worn and weather-beaten countenance, full of energy, and expressive of an iron will; but the gentle wisdom, the deep, broad, tender sympathies, were altogether wanting in Old Blood-and-Thunder's visage; and even if the Great Stone Face had assumed his look of stern command, the milder traits would still have tempered lit.

"This is not the man of prophecy," sighed Ernest to himself, as he made his way out of the throng. "And must the world wait longer yet?"

The mists had congregated about the distant mountain-side, and there were seen the grand and awful features of the Great Stone Face, awful but benignant, as if a mighty angel were sitting among the hills, and enrobing himself in a cloud-vesture of gold and purple. As he looked, Ernest could hardly believe but that a smile beamed over the whole visage, with a radiance still brightening, although without motion of the lips. It was probably the effect of the western sunshine, melting through the thinly diffused vapors that had swept between him and the object that he gazed at. But—as it always did—the aspect of his marvellous friend made Ernest as hopeful as if he had never hoped in vain.

"Fear not, Ernest," said his heart, even as if the Great Face were whispering him,—"fear not, Ernest; he will come."

More years sped swiftly and tranquilly away. Ernest still dwelt in his native valley, and was now a man of middle age. By imperceptible degrees, he had become known among the people. Now, as heretofore, he labored for his bread, and was the same simple hearted man that he had always been. But he had thought and felt so much, he had given so many of the best hours of his life to unworldly hopes for some great good to mankind, that it seemed as though he been talking with the angels, and had imbibed a portion of their wisdom unawares. It was visible in the calm and well considered beneficence of his daily life, the quiet stream of which had made a wide green margin all along its course. Not a day passed by, that the world was not the better because this man, humble as he was, had lived. He never stepped aside from his own path, yet would always reach a blessing to his neighbor. Almost involuntarily, too, he had become a preacher. The pure and high simplicity of his thought, which, as one of its manifestations, took shape in the good deeds that dropped silently from his hand, flowed also forth in speech. He uttered truths that wrought upon and moulded the lives of those who heard him. His auditors, it may be, never suspected that Ernest, their own neighbor and familiar friend, was more than an ordinary man; least of all did Ernest himself suspect it; but, inevitably as the murmur of a rivulet, came thoughts out of his mouth that no other human lips had spoken.

When the people's minds had had a little time to cool, they were ready enough to acknowledge their mistake in imagining a similarity between General Blood-and-Thunder's truculent physiognomy and the benign visage on the mountain-side. But now, again, there were reports and many paragraphs in the newspapers, affirming that the likeness of the Great Stone Face had appeared upon the broad shoulders of a certain eminent statesman. He, like Mr. Gathergold and old Blood-and-Thunder, was a native of the valley, but had left it in his early days, and taken up the trades of law and politics. Instead of the rich man's wealth and the warrior's sword, he had but a tongue, and it was mightier than both together. So wonderfully eloquent was he, that whatever he might choose to say, his auditors had no choice but to believe him; wrong looked like right, and right like wrong; for when it pleased him, he could make a kind of illuminated fog with his mere breath, and obscure the natural daylight with it. His tongue, indeed, was a magic instrument: sometimes it rumbled like the thunder; sometimes it warbled like the sweetest music. It was the blast of war,—the song of peace; and it seemed to have a heart in it, when there was no such matter. In good truth, he was a wondrous man; and when his tongue had acquired him all other imaginable success,—when it had been heard in halls of state, and in the courts of princes and potentates,—after it had made him known all over the world, even as a voice crying from shore to shore,—

it finally persuaded his countrymen to select him for the Presidency. Before this time,—indeed, as soon as he began to grow celebrated, —his admirers had found out the resemblance between him and the Great Stone Face; and so much were they struck by it, that throughout the country this distinguished gentleman was known by the name of Old Stony Phiz. The phrase was considered as giving a highly favorable aspect to his political prospects; for, as is likewise the with the Popedom, nobody ever becomes President without taking a name other than his own.

While his friends were doing their best to make him President, Old Stony Phiz, as he was called, set out on a visit to the valley where he was born. Of course, he had no other object than to shake hands with his fellow-citizens, and neither thought nor cared about any effect which his progress through the country might have upon the election. Magnificent preparations were made to receive the illustrious statesman; a cavalcade of horsemen set forth to meet him at the boundary line of the State, and all the people left their business and gathered along the wayside to see him pass. Among these was Ernest. Though more than once disappointed, as we have seen, he had such a hopeful and confiding nature, that he was always ready to believe in whatever seemed beautiful and good. He kept his heart continually open, and thus was sure to catch the blessing from on high when it should come. So now again, as buoyantly as ever, he went forth to behold the likeness of the Great Stone Face.

The cavalcade came prancing along the road, with a great clattering of hoofs and a mighty cloud of dust, which rose up so dense and high that the visage of the mountain-side was completely hidden from Ernest's eyes. All the great men of the neighborhood were there on horseback; militia officers, in uniform; the member of Congress; the sheriff of the county; the editors of newspapers; and many a farmer, too, had mounted his patient steed, with his Sunday coat upon his back. It really was a very brilliant spectacle, especially as there were numerous banners flaunting over the cavalcade, on some of which were gorgeous portraits of the illustrious statesman and the Great Stone Face, smiling familiarly at one another, like two brothers. If the pictures were to be trusted, the mutual resemblance, it must be confessed, was marvellous. We must not forget to mention that there was a band of music, which made the echoes of the mountains ring and reverberate with the loud triumph of its strains; so that airy and soul thrilling melodies broke out among all the heights and hollows, as if every nook of his native valley had found a voice, to welcome the distinguished guest. But the grandest effect was when the far-off mountain precipice flung back the music; for then the Great Stone Face itself seemed to be swelling the triumphant chorus, in acknowledgment that, at length, the man of prophecy was come.

All this while the people were throwing up their hats and shouting, with enthusiasm so contagious that the heart of Ernest kindled up, and he likewise threw up his hat, and shouted, as loudly as the loudest, "Huzza for the great man! Huzza for Old Stony Phiz!" But as yet he had not seen him.

"Here he is, now!" cried those who stood near Ernest. "There! There! Look at Old Stony Phiz and then at the Old Man of the Mountain, and see if they are not as like as two twin brothers!"

In the midst of all this gallant array came an open barouche, drawn by four white horses; and in the barouche, with his massive head uncovered, sat the illustrious statesman, Old Stony Phiz himself.

"Confess it," said one of Ernest's neighbors to him, "the Great Stone Face has met its match at last!"

Now, it must be owned that, at his first glimpse of the countenance which was bowing and smiling from the barouche, Ernest did fancy that there was a resemblance between it and the old familiar face upon the mountain-side. The brow, with its massive depth and loftiness and all the other features, indeed, were boldly and strongly hewn, as if in emulation of a more than heroic, of a Titanic model. But the sublimity and stateliness, the grand expression of a divine sympathy, that illuminated the mountain visage and etherealized its ponderous granite substance into spirit, might here be sought in vain. Something had been originally left out, or had departed. And therefore the marvelously gifted statesman had always a weary gloom in the deep caverns of his eyes, as of a child that has outgrown its playthings or a man of mighty faculties and little aims, whose life, with all its high performances, was vague and empty, because no high purpose had endowed it with reality.

Still, Ernest's neighbor was thrusting his elbow into his side, and pressing him for an answer.

"Confess! confess! Is not he the very picture of your Old Man of the Mountain?"

"No!" said Ernest, bluntly, "I see little or no likeness."

"Then so much the worse for the Great Stone Face!" answered his neighbor; and again he set up a shout for Old Stony Phiz.

But Ernest turned away, melancholy, and almost despondent: for this was the saddest of his disappointments, to behold a man who might have fulfilled the prophecy, and had not willed to do so. Meantime, the cavalcade, the banners, the music, and the barouches swept past him, with the vociferous crowd in the rear, leaving the dust to settle down, and the Great Stone Face to be revealed again, with the grandeur that it had worn for untold centuries.

"Lo, here I am, Ernest!" the benign lips seemed to say. "I have waited longer than thou, and am not yet weary. Fear not; the man will come."

The years hurried onward, treading in their haste on one another's heels. And now they began to bring white hairs, and scatter them over the head of Ernest; they made reverend wrinkles across his forehead, and furrows in his cheeks. He was an aged man. But not in vain had he grown old: more than the white hairs on his head were the sage thoughts in his mind; his wrinkles and furrows were inscriptions that Time had graved, and in which he had written legends of wisdom that had been tested by the tenor of a life. And Ernest had ceased to be obscure. Unsought for, undesired, had come the fame which so many seek, and made him known in the great world, beyond the limits of the valley in which he had dwelt so quietly. College professors, and even the active men of cities, came from far to see and converse with Ernest; for the report had gone abroad that this simple husbandman had ideas unlike those of other men, not gained from books, but of a higher tone,—a tranquil and familiar majesty, as if he had been talking with the angels as his daily friends. Whether it were sage, statesman, or philanthropist, Ernest received these visitors with the gentle sincerity that had characterized him from boyhood, and spoke freely with them of whatever came uppermost, or lay deepest in his heart or their own. While they talked together, his face would kindle, unawares, and shine upon them, as with a mild evening light. Pensive with the fullness of such discourse, his guests took leave and went their way; and passing up the valley, paused to look at the Great Stone Face, imagining that they had seen its likeness in a human countenance, but could not remember where.

While Ernest had been growing up and growing old, a bountiful Providence had granted a new poet to this earth. He, likewise, was a native of the valley, but had spent the greater part of his life at a distance from that romantic region, pouring out his sweet music amid the bustle and din of cities. Often, however, did the mountains which had been familiar to him in his childhood lift their snowy peaks into the clear atmosphere of his poetry. Neither was the Great Stone Face forgotten, for the poet had celebrated it in an ode, which was grand enough to have been uttered by its own majestic lips. This man of genius, we may say, had come down from heaven with wonderful endowments. If he sang of a mountain, the eyes of all mankind beheld a mightier grandeur reposing on its breast, or soaring to its summit, than had before been seen there. If his theme were a lovely lake, a celestial smile had now been thrown over it to gleam forever on its surface. If it were the vast old sea, even the deep immensity of its dread bosom seemed to swell the higher, as if moved by the emotions of the song. Thus the world assumed another and a better aspect from the hour that the poet blessed it with his happy eyes. The Creator had bestowed him, as the last best touch to his own handiwork. Creation was not finished till the poet came to interpret, and so complete it.

The effect was no less high and beautiful, when his human brethren were the subject of his verse. The man or woman, sordid with the common dust of life, who crossed his daily path, and the little child who played in it, were glorified if he beheld them in his mood of poetic faith. He showed the golden links of the great chain that intertwined them with an angelic kindred; he brought out the hidden traits of a celestial birth that made them worthy of such kin. Some, indeed, there were, who thought to show the soundness of their judgment by affirming that all the beauty and dignity of the natural world existed only in the poet's fancy. Let such men speak for themselves, who undoubtedly appear to have been spawned forth by Nature with a contemptuous bitterness; she having plastered them up out of her refuse stuff, after all the swine were made. As respects all things else, the poet's ideal was the truest truth.

The songs of this poet found their way to Ernest. He read them after his customary toil, seated on the bench before his cottage-door, where for such a length of time he had filled his repose with thought, by gazing at the Great Stone Face. And now as he read stanzas that caused the soul to thrill within him, he lifted his eyes to the vast countenance beaming on him so benignantly.

"O majestic friend," he murmured, addressing the Great Stone Face, "is not this man worthy to resemble thee?"

The face seemed to smile, but answered not a word.

Now it happened that the poet, though he dwelt so far away, had not only heard of Ernest, but had meditated much upon his character, until he deemed nothing so desirable as to meet this man, whose untaught wisdom walked hand in hand with the noble simplicity of his life. One summer morning, therefore, he took passage by the railroad, and, in the decline of the afternoon, alighted from the cars at no great distance from Ernest's cottage. The great hotel, which had formerly been the palace of Mr. Gathergold, was close at hand, but the poet, with his carpetbag on his arm, inquired at once where Ernest dwelt, and was resolved to be accepted as his guest.

Approaching the door, he there found the good old man, holding a volume in his hand, which alternately he read, and then, with a finger between the leaves, looked lovingly at the Great Stone Face.

"Good evening," said the poet. "Can you give a traveller a night's lodging?"

"Willingly," answered Ernest; and then he added, smiling, "Methinks I never saw the Great Stone Face look so hospitably at a stranger."

The poet sat down on the bench beside him, and he and Ernest talked together. Often had the poet held intercourse with the wittiest and the wisest, but never before with a man like Ernest, whose thoughts and feelings gushed up with such a natural feeling, and who made great truths so familiar by his simple utterance of them. Angels, as had been so often said, seemed to have wrought with him at his labor in the fields; angels seemed to have sat with him by the fireside; and, dwelling with angels as friend with friends, he had imbibed the sublimity of their ideas, and imbued it with the sweet and lowly charm of household words. So thought the poet. And Ernest, on the other hand, was moved and agitated by the living images which the poet flung out of his mind, and which peopled all the air about the cottage-door with shapes of beauty, both gay and pensive. The sympathies of these two men instructed them with a profounder sense than either could have attained alone. Their minds accorded into one strain, and made delightful music which neither of them could have claimed as all his own, nor distinguished his own share from the other's. They led one another, as it were, into a high pavilion of their thoughts, so remote, and hitherto so dim, that they had never entered it before, and so beautiful that they desired to be there always. As Ernest listened to the poet, he imagined that the Great Stone Face was bending forward to listen too. He gazed earnestly into the poet's glowing eyes.

"Who are you, my strangely gifted guest?" he said.

The poet laid his finger on the volume that Ernest had been reading.

"You have read all these poems," said he. "You know me, then,—for I wrote them."

Again, and still more earnestly than before, Ernest examined the poet's features; then turned towards the Great Stone Face; then back, with an uncertain aspect, to his guest. But his countenance fell; he shook his head, and sighed.

"Wherefore are you sad?" inquired the poet.

"Because," replied Ernest, "all through life I have awaited the fulfillment of a prophecy; and, when I read these poems, I hoped that it might be fulfilled in you."

"You hoped," answered the poet, faintly smiling, "to find in me the likeness of the Great Stone Face. And you are disappointed, as formerly with Mr. Gathergold, and old Blood-and-Thunder, and Old Stony Phiz. Yes, Ernest, it is my doom. You must add my name to the illustrious three, and record another failure of your hopes. For—in shame and sadness do I speak it, Ernest—I am not worthy to be typified by yonder benign and majestic image."

"And why?" asked Ernest. He pointed to the volume. "Are not those thoughts divine?"

"They have a strain of the Divinity," replied the poet. "You can hear in them the far-off echo of a heavenly song. But my life, dear Ernest, has not corresponded with my thought. I have had grand dreams, but they have been only dreams, because I have lived —and that, too, by my own choice—among poor and mean realities. Sometimes, even—shall I dare to say it? I lack faith in the grandeur, the beauty, and the goodness, which my own works are said to have made more evident in nature and in human life. Why, then, pure seeker of the good and true, shouldst thou hope to find me, in yonder image of the divine?"

The poet spoke sadly, and his eyes were dim with tears. So, likewise, were those of Ernest.

At the hour of sunset, as had long been his frequent custom, Ernest was to discourse to an assemblage of the neighboring inhabitants in the open air. He and the poet, arm in arm, still talking together as they went along, proceeded to the spot. It was a small nook among the hills, with a gray precipice behind, the stern front of which was relieved by the pleasant foliage of many creeping plants that made a tapestry for the naked rock, by hanging their festoons from all its rugged angles. At a small elevation above the ground, set in a rich framework of verdure, there appeared. a niche, spacious enough to admit a human figure, with freedom for such gestures as spontaneously accompany earnest thought and genuine emotion. Into this natural pulpit Ernest ascended, and threw a look of familiar kindness around upon his audience. They stood, or sat, or reclined upon the grass, as seemed good to each, with the departing sunshine falling obliquely over them, and mingling its subdued cheerfulness with the solemnity of a grove of ancient trees, beneath and amid the boughs of which the golden rays were constrained to pass. In another direction was seen the Great Stone Face, with the same cheer, combined with the same solemnity, in its benignant aspect.

Ernest began to speak, giving to the people of what was in his heart and mind. His words had power, because they accorded with his thoughts; and his thoughts had reality and depth, because they harmonized with the life which he had always lived. It was not mere breath that this preacher uttered; they were the words of life, because a life of good deeds and holy love was melted into them. Pearls, pure and rich, had been dissolved into this precious draught. The poet, as he listened, felt that the being and character of Ernest were a nobler strain of poetry than he had ever written. His eyes glistening with tears, he gazed reverentially at the venerable man, and said within himself that never was there an aspect so worthy of a prophet and a sage as that mild, sweet, thoughtful countenance, with the glory of white hair diffused about it. At a distance, but distinctly to be seen, high up in the golden light of the setting sun, appeared the Great Stone Face, with hoary mists around it, like the white hairs around the brow of Ernest. Its look of grand beneficence seemed to embrace the world.

At that moment, in sympathy with a thought which he was about to utter, the face of Ernest assumed a grandeur of expression, so imbued with benevolence, that the poet, by an irresistible impulse, threw his arms aloft and shouted,—

"Behold! Behold! Ernest is himself the likeness of the Great Stone Face!"

Then all the people looked and saw that what the deep-sighted poet said was true. The prophecy was—fulfilled. But Ernest, having finished what he had to say, took the poet's arm, and walked slowly homeward, still hoping that some wiser and better man than himself would by and by appear, bearing a resemblance to the GREAT STONE FACE.

THE END

A Play & Poetry

The Great Stone Face
(a play)

Poetry

THE GREAT STONE FACE

The Great Stone Face
A Fifth Grade Play

The handwritten manuscript for this elementary school play was found among the papers of Frances Ann Johnson Hancock (see page 175), in the Dartmouth College Library. One student recalls writing this little play in 1945 when she was a student in Mrs. Hancock's fifth grade class in Littleton, New Hampshire. Mrs. Hancock is remembered as an excellent teacher who used many innovative ways to make the schoolwork more interesting for her young students. References to "Song" are to the song, "Old Man of the Mountains" included with the poetry, page 175. The authors of this play and the original 1945 cast have been identified as follows: Announcer: Nancy Stevens. Ernest the Boy: George Lewis. Ernest-the-Man: Carbee Roach. Gathergold: Jimmy Southand. Blood-and-Thunder: Roddy Blaisdell. Stony Phiz: Frank Guider. The Poet: John McDonald. The Voice: Nelson Kinne. Widow: Nancy Ross. Child: Sally Marsh. Coachman: John Tunney. Flagbearer: Laddie Carmen. Signbearer: John Bigelow. 1st Villager: Nancy St. Lawrence. 2nd Villager: Eleanor Rowe. 4th Villager: Shirley Walters. Other Villagers: Elene Douglas, Sidney Spreadbury, Margaret Welch, Allvin Leonard, Julia Roberts, Claudette Woodbury and Roland Soule. Unidentified members of the cast include: 3rd Villager: Dotty P. 5th Villager: Nelson K. 6th Villager: Barbara D., and Villagers: Joan, Henry, Margaret P., and Charlotte. Many of the co-authors and actors continue to live in the White Mountains—in the shadow of the Old Man of the Mountains. The play is reprinted courtesy of the Dartmouth College Library.

All scenes take place outside of Ernest's cottage beside Profile Lake.

ANNOUNCER: Nathaniel Hawthorne wrote "The Story of the Great Stone Face." We are going to present it as a play.

The story takes place in Franconia Notch beneath the Old Man of the Mountain. It is the story of a little boy who grew up loving the famous Profile and hoping he would someday see the likeness of the noble face. He waited many years but at last the likeness was found.

SCENE I

THE PROPHECY

Time: Ernest was a young boy.

Mother. [*Knitting*]: It is nearly suppertime and Ernest should be here anytime. He is a good boy. I am sure no Mother ever had a better son. [*Looks at Profile*] Maybe he is good because he loves the Great Stone Face so much.

Ernest. [*Enters, gives mother bouquet*] Hello, Mother. Here is a bouquet for you. I have been for a walk around Profile Lake.

Mother. [*Admiring flowers*] Thank you Ernest. You are always doing kind things.

Ernest. [*Looking at Profile*] How beautiful it is today! I wish he could speak. Please tell me the Prophecy again.

Mother. [*Has Ernest sit at her feet.*] The old Prophecy claims that some day a boy born in our valley will return and prove to be the likeness of the Great Stone Face.

Ernest. [*Stands, looks up.*] Oh, Mother, I hope that I may live to see him. I'm sure I'll love him dearly!

Mother. [*Stands, puts knitting away.*] I hope you may live to see him Ernest. He'll be a good man. [*Song.*]

SCENE II

GATHERGOLD

Time: A few years later.

Ernest. [*Very excited.*] Oh, Mother, they say that Gathergold is the likeness of the Great Stone Face! And he will arrive in the valley today!

Mother. Hurry and comb your hair Ernest. He may come at any moment now. [*Ernest dashes off.*] Here he comes now, Ernest! He must be very wealthy! [*Ernest dashes in.*] See the beautiful coach!

Ernest. And what handsome clothes! And see! All the village people are following him!

Mother. Listen, they are singing "The Old Man of the Mountain" song to him. [*Song, very soft.*]

Ernest. Must be they think he really is the likeness.

Mother. Oh, he's stopping here! [*Stand and go.*]

Gathergold. [*Enters with villagers.*] Hrumph! Hrumph! Well! [*Looks at Profile.*] So that's what I'm supposed to look like!

Ernest. [*Doubtfully.*] Are you really the great Gathergold?

Gathergold. Well, if I'm not, then who am I?! Of course I'm Gathergold! I have more wealth than I can count!

1st Villager. Yes, he says he has riches from all over the world.

Ernest. But riches don't make a good, great man.

2nd Villager. No, but they do make a man famous and important!

Widow. [*Holding out hands.*] If you are so wealthy, won't you please give to a poor widow and her child?

Gathergold. Bah! A copper I give to you, [*tosses coin*] but no one gets my silver and gold!

Child. But you have so much!

Gathergold. And I intend to hang onto it!

All villagers. Yea! Yea! It belongs to our great Gathergold.

Coachman. Your coach is waiting, noble Gathergold!

Gathergold. Fine! I must go now to my castle. Well, it's nice to be famous as well as rich.

Villagers. Three cheers for the great Gathergold! [*Follow him off.*]

Ernest. [*Looks at Profile*] Gathergold is not the likeness, noble face.

Voice. No, but fear not Ernest. He will come.

SCENE III

BLOOD-AND-THUNDER

Time: After Ernest becomes a man.

Ernest. [*Now a man.*] I wonder why the likeness doesn't come. Maybe that brave and honored soldier old Blood-and-Thunder is the right one. He returns to the valley today. [*Hears singing*] Oh, that must be the villagers coming with him now.

3rd Villager. [*Runs ahead of others.*] He's here, Ernest. The likeness is here!

Ernest. Is he coming here to see The Great Stone Face? [*3rd Villager nods.*]

Flag Carrier. [*Entering.*] Hail! Blood-and-Thunder! The likeness is here at last!

Blood-and-Thunder. [*Followed by villagers.*] Ha! Ha! Ha! So you think I look like the old boy up on the mountain! Well, maybe I do! Maybe I do! But we're not much alike. I've been all over the world and he never went anywhere in his life! Ha! Ha! Ha!

4th Villager. You must be a very brave man, Blood-and-Thunder. You have probably won in many battles.

Villagers. Yea! Yea! Blood-and-Thunder is the likeness.

Flag Bearer. Come, let us celebrate with feasting and dancing! [*All go off.*]

Ernest. But courage in battle is not enough, and Blood-and-Thunder brags about his courage. Will the likeness ever come?

Voice. Fear not, Ernest, he will come.

SCENE IV

OLD STONY PHIZ

Time: Years later.

Ernest. [*Discouraged.*] They say that our candidate for President, Old Stony Phiz is really the likeness at last. I hope he is not a disappointment like Gathergold and Blood-and-Thunder. It is nearly time for him to arrive. [*Song, Old Man of the*

The Old Man of The Mountain, W. Hamilton Gibson. Included in *The Heart of the White Mountains* by Samuel A. Drake. New York, 1882. From the author's collection.

Mountain. Sign bearer leads Stony Phiz and villagers to stage.]

5th Villager. [*When everyone is quiet.*] Ernest, we have at last found the likeness! We have brought him to you because we know how long you have waited.

Ernest. [*Shaking Hands.*] Welcome to our valley, Stony Phiz. We are honored to have a presidential candidate visit us. Won't you please speak to us about your plans for our country.

Stony Phiz. [*Very stiff and lofty.*] My dea Ernest and other friends. It is a great honna to be here. It is also an honna to be called the likeness of the Great Stone Face. Howeva the hona leaves out the fact that the Profile can not speak, while I am famous everywhea! My words are famous around the world. When I go to Washington, I shall rememba what dea people you are! And I shall rememba how dea you have been to honna me! Thank you! [*Bows.*]

Villagers. Yea! Yea! Old Stony Phiz! [*All go off but Ernest.*]

Ernest. [*Sadly.*] No, he is not the likeness. He may have a silverer tongue but he lacks something! Will the likeness ever come?

Voice. Fear not, Ernest. He **will** come!

SCENE V

THE POET

Time: When Ernest was an old man.

Ernest. [*Now an old man.*] I have waited all these years for the likeness. I would lose faith, but the Great Stone Face has said he will come. I am getting old. They call me the Old Man of the Mountains, and they sing that song to me whenever they come to call. [*Hears singing.*] Ah, they are coming now! [*Villagers and poet enter.*] Welcome, friends!

6th Villager. Ernest, we have brought you a guest. He is the well-known poet whose beautiful poems you enjoy so much. [*Poet and Ernest shake hands.*]

Ernest. Welcome poet friend. Your poems are beautiful. Maybe a man who writes such great thoughts deserves to be the likeness of the Great Stone Face.

Poet. No Ernest, I am sorry, but I have not lived as nobly as I have written. The likeness should be a man who is kind, generous, modest, and loved by all.

Ernest. But I have waited so long for the likeness!

Poet. [*Suddenly excited.*] Wait, Ernest! Look no farther for the likeness!

Ernest. What do you mean, poet friend?

Poet. I meant that you are the likeness. You have lived with the Great Stone Face all your life, and your face shows his strength and goodness. For it is true that we have become like what we love. [*Turns to Villagers.*] Behold, Ernest is the likeness of The Great Stone Face!

Villagers. Three cheers for our beloved friend, Ernest. *He* is the likeness! [*All sing.*]

The End.

POETRY

To The Stone Face
John W. Condon

A Summer in New Hampshire: Out-of-Door Songs for All Who Love the Granite State was a collection of poems compiled by Mary Currier and published in 1903. John W. Condon was identified as being from Manchester, New Hampshire.

Braving the javelins of the thunder-god,
　　Through each succeeding century the same.
　　Careless alike of good or evil fame,
Permitting not thy lofty head to nod
Whether the light or darkness kiss the sod,
　　How well may fickle man be taught of thee
　　The long, hard lesson of true constancy!
The rugged paths the martyr's feet have trod
Perhaps were smoother for that stoic will
　　Which, buffeted by Fate, refused to yield,
　　But met each fresh attack, and kept the field
With head erect, and stayed to conquer still.
　　So in this face of solid rock we find
　　A silent tutor for the thoughtful mind.

White Mts. N. H., Old Man of the Mountain. Postcard. From the author's collection.

The Old Man of the Mountain
Moody Currier

Moody Currier was born in 1806 on the family farm in Boscawen, New Hampshire. He attended the Hopkinton Academy and then studied at Dartmouth College, a member of the class of 1834. Currier's first career was as a teacher, first at his old school, Hopkinton Academy and then as the principal of the Lowell, Massachusetts, High School. However, teaching was not to be the Currier's lifelong avocation. He became a lawyer and was the cashier of the Amoskeag Bank in Manchester when that institution was formed. He became a successful and wealthy businessman and was elected Governor of New Hampshire in 1885. His mansion in Manchester was testimony to his financially successful career. After both Moody Currier and his wife had died, the mansion and estate were left to be used for the benefit of the City of Manchester and the establishment of an art museum, The Currier Art Gallery.

Thy home is on the mountain's brow,
Where clouds hang thick, and tempests blow.
Unnumbered years, with silent tread,
Have passed above thy rocky head;
Whilst round these heights the beating storm
Has worn, with rage, thy deathless form:
And yet thou sit'st, unmoved, alone,
Upon this ancient mountain home.
Long as these towering peaks shall stand,
So wondrous great, so nobly grand,
Serene, on high, that face of thine,
Shall mock the wasting hand of time,
Whilst all that live shall pass away,
And all the tribes of earth decay.
Old Man! thy face of rock sublime
Looks back, through years, to ancient time,
When first the forming hand divine

Reared up this rocky home of thine,
And from the lowest depths of earth
These mountain forms had first their birth;
When on these shaggy heights imprest,
Thy changeless form was doomed to rest.

Then tell me, man of silent tongue,
How first the heavens and earth begun;
If all this bright and shining frame,
With all these worlds, from nothing came;
If all these starry orbs of light,
That glitter on the robes of night,
And fill creation's vast expanse,
Began at once their mystic dance;
Or, if from mists that dimly shine,
Worlds spring to light by power divine,
Till all the radiant fields afar
Shall beam with light of sun and star.
And tell me where, in depths profound,
The primal germs of earth were found,
Which, rising up from realms of death,
Instinct with life and vital breath,
Have formed this wondrous orb we see
Of hill and plain and waste of sea,
Where busy life, with forming power,
Unfolds itself in plant and flower,
And upward still, with widening plan,
Kindles the pulse of beast and man.
And tell me whence, from earth or heaven,
That living spark to man was given,
Which shines in God's eternal day,
When all things else shall pass away.

The Old Man of the Mountain by Moonlight. On a recent evening the Old Man permitted an artist to draw this never before seen profile of the other side of his face. All other pictures have shown the left side, but here we can see the right side of his face for the first time. During the entire session with the artist The Old Man was very quiet and said nothing. Picture courtesy of a friend of the Old Man.

The Old Man
Robert F. Doane

In 1939 The North Country Ministers' and Laymen's Association published *A North Country Anthology,* a short collection of poetry about New Hampshire, which included two poems by Robert Doane. The anthology noted that Doane had been thirteen years old when he wrote the poems and that he was from Campton, New Hampshire. Doane was a White Mountain visitor whose family first stayed in a Civilian Conservation Corps campground in Waterville Valley and then in 1939 purchased a small camp that they continue to use. Doane served in the Pacific during World War II, received his degree in Sociology from Haverford College after the war, worked in Mexico for the American Friends Service Committee, and then had a long career in a Philadelphia bookstore of which he noted in 1994, "Books seem to be what I am about."

On the crest of a mighty mountain
　　Looking over the lake below,
A face with a human expression
　　Watches many a century go.

It was made from a mountain of granite
　　With the skill of a sculptor's hand,
And guards the green valley below it
　　As time passes over the land.

At dusk when the birds cease their carols
   And the wind murmurs through the trees,
There's a sense of sadness about you,
   As you stand in the evening breeze.

You feel that a great respect's due him-
   So mighty beneath the blue sky,
There are few who have not been inspired
   By that face as they've passed it by.

And to me, as to Daniel Webster,
   The thought comes now and again
That in the great State of New Hampshire
   The Master of Sculptors makes men.

Old Man of the Mountain
Mary Baker Eddy

Mary Baker Eddy, the founder of the Christian Science Church, was born on July 16, 1821 in Bow, New Hampshire, where the site of the family farmstead is today marked by its stone foundation. She was a deeply religious woman whose organizational and leadership abilities contributed greatly to the success of the church that she founded. As Mrs. Eddy was writing this poem, seated on a rock, several tourists passed her. After introducing themselves, Mrs. Eddy read them her new poem. The tourists were all very impressed, and Mrs. Eddy later sent them a copy. There are two slightly different versions of her poem *Old Man of the Mountain* which she wrote when she visited the White Mountains as a young woman. (The different versions of Mrs. Eddy's poem may be found in the following sources: *Saving the Great Stone Face* by Frances Ann Johnson Hancock, *Old Man of the Mountain* by Leon W. Anderson and *Gems for You: From New Hampshire* compiled by F. A. Moore and published in 1850. The differences are shown in the footnotes.)

Gigantic sire, unfallen still thy crest![1]
Primeval dweller where the wild winds rest!
Beyond the ken of mortal e'er to tell
What power sustains thee in thy rock-bound cell.

Or if, when first creation vast began,[2]
And far the universal fiat ran,[3]
"Let there be light" — from chaos dark set free,
Ye rose, a monument of Deity.

Proud from yon cloud-crowned height to look henceforth[4]
On insignificance that peoples earth,
Recalling oft the bitter draft which turns[5]
The mind to meditate on what it learns.

Stern, passionless, no soul those looks betray;
Though kindred rocks, to sport at mortal clay —
Much as the chisel of the sculptor's art[6]
"Plays round the head, but comes not to the heart."[7]

Ah, who can fathom thee! Ambitious man,
Like a trained falcon in the Gallic van,
Guided and led, can never reach to thee
With all the strength of weakness — vanity![8]

Great as thou art, and paralled by none,
Admired by all, still art thou drear and lone!
The moon looks down upon thine exiled height,
The stars, so cold, so glitteringly bright,[9]

On wings of morning gladly flit away,
Yield to the sun's more genial, mighty ray;[10]
The white waves kiss the murmuring rill —
But thy deep silence is unbroken still.

---

[1] Gigantic size, unfallen still that crest!
[2] Or if, when erst creation vast began,
[3] And loud the universal fiat ran,
[4] Proud from yon cloud-crowned height thou peerest forth
[5] Recalling oft the bitter drug which turns
[6] Like to the chisel of the sculptor's art
[7] "Play round the head, but come not to the heart."
[8] With e'en the strength of weakness — vanity !
[9] The stars, so mildly, spiritually bright
[10] To mix with their more genial, mighty ray;

The Old Man of the Mountain
George Bancroft Griffith

George Bancroft Griffith was born in Newburyport, Massachusetts, on February 28, 1841. Griffith married Anne Howe of Bradford, New Hampshire, and they had six children. In 1871 he moved to Newport, New Hampshire, and three years later he moved to Lempster, New Hampshire, where he wrote poetry.

Shaped of God's finger from the dust,
    Even as Adam was of old,
That we of fortitude and trust
    Here in thy presence might be told—

Not as by letters carven deep
    Into the Table of the Law,
But by thine image o'er the steep,
    Speechless, yet waking holy awe.

Eternal teacher! left to bear
    Among the lofty clouds of heaven
Unwritten truths wrought with such care,—
    The bread of thought in cold stone given!

Daily cleaving through cloud and mist,
    Calm as 'midst passing rents of blue;
By many a sunset's last rays kissed
    Kindest of sitters when artists view.

Chasten, rebuke our feeble souls!
    In golden fortitude abide
Long as the earth in its orbit rolls;
    Thy mountain gate still open wide!

EAST LEMPSTER, N. H.

5:—OLD MAN OF THE MOUNTAIN BY MOONLIGHT, WHITE MTS., N. H.

Old Man of the Mountain by Moonlight, White Mts., N. H. Postcard. From the author's collection.

Franconia's Profile
George Bancroft Griffith

They hail the Rocky Mountains and the Garden of the Gods,
Up the Alps and Andes yearly many a weary tourist plods,
And, 'midst panoramic changes, over stony stairways long,
They have told us of their climbing in cold prose and melting
    song;
But my happiest moment gilding, the most thankful since my
    birth,
Shone the sun on in New England, the dearest spot on earth.
It was when in manhood's vigor I beheld the Face of Stone,
And Franconia's pines all murmured, "See him there, upon his
    throne!"
Yes, 't was summer; all the valleys were a mass of leafy bloom;
Form and color dazzled vision, there was not a hint of gloom;
Echo lake, in restful beauty, like a polished mirror shone;
In the heart of nature's wonders, rapt, I stood as if alone.
Never, never will that moment from my mem'ry fade away,
And its rapture, sweet and sacred, will make calm my dying
    day,
For I knew the Hand that fashioned such an image in a breath
Made all things and ruled wisely over life and over death.
With the thought, the lips, rock-sculptured, lost their stern-
    ness, and the face
For a flash smiled kindly on me with benignity and grace,
And I stood with clasped hands, dreaming where a thousand
    splendors shone;
Hope's rainbow brightly glistened above the face of stone;
Franconia's pines breathed softer, while a voice said, "From
    the sod
The trusting soul soars upward to the bosom of its God!"

The Old Man of the Mountain
George Bancroft Griffith

Must thou, O figure stern, yet grand!
  The glory of our Northern clime,
Bow to the touch of human hand,
  Or mandate of relentless time?
Some bold cliff-climber, I am told.
  An iron clamp would fasten now
E'en where the sunset's purest gold
  Hath for long ages bathed that brow!

That scarred, aye, battered by the blast,
  Thy dissolution is at hand-
Thou, in such wondrous fashion cast,
  Thou, by Almighty Wisdom planned!
The rising sun upon thy face
  Has smiled for æons, and the moon
Has silvered it with chastened grace:
  Oh! say not thou must perish soon!

Who knows what race an idol made
  And hailed thee from the lake below,
Ere Red Man saw Franconia's shade,
  Or Saxon felt our breezes blow!
Perchance thy lofty brow was fanned
  By the first summer's freshest air,
And the first rainbow from God's hand
  Curved in transcendent beauty there!

Think of the dusky chiefs who gazed
   With awe upon thy stately form;
As the Great Spirit thee have praised,
   Or god of stone who braved the storm.
Think of the thousands glad to turn
   From Fashion's shrine to look on thee;
The countless throng who still may yearn
   To contemplate thy majesty!

Man of the Mountain! hold thy own!
   Our race for centuries yet unborn
Would love to see thee on thy throne,
   Among the Crystal Hills at morn!
Long may the eagle's eye delight
   To scan thy features, still sublime;
The dawn's first beam and sunset light
   Kiss thy gray image, saved by time!

Old Man of The Mountains *(a song)*

Frances Ann Johnson Hancock

Mrs. Hancock, a lifelong resident of the White Mountains, was born in Whitefield, New Hampshire, on June 10, 1900. After graduating from Plymouth Normal School in 1920, she began a teaching career of thirty-five years in the public schools of northern New Hampshire. In 1961 she married Frank R. Hancock. Mrs. Hancock died in Littleton, New Hampshire, on October 11, 1979.

During her lifetime Mrs. Hancock published poetry and booklets about New Hampshire and its attractions, and in 1926 she published a song about the Old Man of the Mountain. She was associated with many northern New Hampshire activities including the 1955 celebrations in Franconia Notch where President Eisenhower was the featured speaker commemorating the 150th discovery of the Profile. Before her death she had nearly completed her book *Saving the Great Stone Face: The Chronicle of The Old Man of the Mountain.* The book was published in 1984.

Great stone visage, rich in birth and story,
Silent tribute of unchanging glory
Sharp against ethereal blue,
Mystery of sages,
Where the hands that fashioned you,
King of countless ages?

Somber mountains echo back your thunder,
Thousands seek you, wrapped in speechless wonder,
'Round your head in transient mist,
Like a halo clinging,
As by breath of angels kissed,
Fleecy clouds are winging.

REFRAIN:

Old Man of the mountains,
Proud, noble, supreme!
So constant your vigil,
So sacred your dream!
Lips firm in their justice,
Eyes fearlessly true.
Old Man of the Mountains,
We find God Himself in you!

Great Stone Face

Frances Ann Johnson Hancock

Within a small, tree-shadowed space
I can look up and see a Face
Ice-chiseled long ago.
If I desert that favored sphere,
The noble features disappear
And only ledges show.

It all depends on where I stand
If shapeless rock or something grand
Is visible to me.
And what I choose to keep in view
Becomes a part of all I do
And all I hope to be.

I'll have to choose with equal care
The stand I take in Life, for there
Within my little place
I'll either see just rock and sky
And never know or wonder why,
Or I'll behold a Face!

Franconia Mountain Notch
Harry Hibbard

Harry Hibbard's poem *Franconia Mountain Notch* was originally published in the *Democratic Review* in April 1839. When the poem was re-printed in one anthology of New Hampshire poetry, an editorial note stated that the poem "has been extensively read and justly admired." In 1912, when Eugene Musgrove edited and published *The White Hills in Poetry: An Anthology* he included three verses of Hibbard's poem, but they were printed as three very separate poems with no mention that they were part of a much longer work.

Hibbard was born in Concord, Vermont, on June 1, 1816. In 1835 he graduated from Dartmouth College. An attorney, Hibbard served in the New Hampshire House of Representatives where he was the Speaker from 1844 to 1845. Between 1846 and 1849 he served in the State Senate, being Senate President in 1849. He then served in the United States Congress from 1849 to 1855. Hibbard lived in Lancaster and then later in Bath, New Hampshire, where he died on July 28, 1873.

The blackening hills close round: the beetling cliff
On either hand towers to the upper sky.
I pass the lonely inn; the yawning rift
Grows narrower still, until the passer-by
Beholds himself walled in by mountains high,
Like everlasting barriers, which frown
Around, above, in awful majesty:
Still on, the expanding chasm deepens down,
Into a vast abyss which circling mountains crown.

The summer air is cooler, fresher, here,
The breeze is hushed, and all is calm and still;
Above, a strip of the blue heaven's clear
Cerulean is stretched from hill to hill,
Through which the sun's short transit can distill
No breath of fainting sultriness; the soul

Imbued with love of nature's charms, can fill
Itself with meditation here, and hold
Communion deep with all that round it doth unfold.

Thou reader of these lines, who dost inherit
That love of earth's own loveliness which flings
A glow of chastened feeling o'er the spirit,
And lends creation half its colorings
Of light and beauty; who from living things
Dost love to 'scape to that beatitude
Which from converse with secret nature springs,
Fly to this green and shady solitude,
High hills, clear streams, blue lakes, and everlasting wood.

And as thou musest mid these mountains wild,
Their grandeur thy rapt soul will penetrate,
Till with thyself thou wilt be reconciled,
If not with man; thy thoughts will emulate
Their calm sublime, thy little passions, hate,
Envying and bitterness, if such be found
Within thy breast, these scenes will dissipate,
And lend thy mind a tone of joy profound,
An impress from the grand and mighty scenes around.

Here doth not wake that thrill of awe; that feeling
Of stern sublimity, which overpowers
The mind and sense of him whose foot is scaling
The near White Mountain Notch's giant towers;
Here is less grandeur but more beauty; bowers
For milder, varied pleasure; in the sun
Blue ponds and streams are glancing, fringed with flowers;
There all is vast and overwhelming; one
Is Lafayette, the other, matchless Washington!

Great names! presiding spirits of each scene,
Which here their mountain namesakes overlook;
'Tis well to keep their memories fresh and green
By thus inscribing them within the book
Of earth's enduring records, where will look
Our children's children; till the crumbling hand
Of time wastes all things; every verdant nook
And every crag of these proud hills shall stand
Their glory's emblems o'er our proud and happy land!

Where a tall post beside the road displays
Its lettered arm, pointing the traveller's eye,
Through the small opening mid the green birch trees,
Toward yonder mountain summit towering high,
There pause: what doth thy anxious gaze espy?
An abrupt crag hung from the mountain's brow!
Look closer! scan that bare, sharp cliff on high;
Aha! the wondrous shape bursts on thee now!
A perfect human face—neck, chin, mouth, nose and brow!

And full and plain those features are displayed,
Thus profiled forth against the clear, blue sky,
As though some sculptor's chisel here had made
This fragment of colossal imagery,
The compass of his plastic art to try.
From the curved neck up to the shaggy hair
That shoots in pine trees from the head on high,
All, all is perfect; no illusions there
To cheat the expecting eye with fancied forms of air.

Most wondrous vision! the broad earth hath not
Through all her bounds an object like to thee,
That traveller e'er recorded, nor a spot
More fit to stir the poet's phantasy.

Gray Old Man of the Mountain, awfully
There from thy wreath of clouds thou dost uprear
Those features grand, the same eternally;
Lone dwellers mid the hills! with gaze austere
Thou lookest down, methinks, on all below thee here!

And curious travellers have descried the trace
Of the sage Franklin's physiognomy
In that most grave and philosophic face;
If it be true, Old Man, that we do see
Sage Franklin's countenance, thou indeed must be
A learned philosopher, most wise and staid,
From all that thou hast had a chance to see,
Since earth began. Here thou, too, oft hast played
With lightnings, glancing frequent round thy rugged head.

Thou sawest the tawny Indian's light canoe
Glide o'er the pond that glistens at thy feet,
And the white hunter first emerge to view
From up yon ravine where the mountains meet,
To scare the red man from his ancient seat,
Where he had roamed for ages, wild and free.
The motley stream which since from every state
And clime through this wild vale pours ceaselessly,
Travellers, gay tourists, all have been a theme to thee.

In thee the simple-minded Indian saw
The image of his more benignant God,
And viewed with deep and reverential awe
The spot where the Great Spirit made abode;

When storms obscured thee, and red lightnings glowed
From the dark clouds oft gathered round thy face,
He saw thy form in anger veiled, nor rowed
His birchen bark, nor sought the wild deer chase,
Till thy dark frown had passed, and sunshine filled its place.

Oh! that some bard would rise, true heir of glory,
With the full power of heavenly poesy,
To gather up each old romantic story
That lingers round these scenes in memory,
And consecrate to immortality;
Some western Scott, within whose bosom thrills
That fire which burneth to eternity,
To pour his spirit o'er these mighty hills,
And make them classic ground, thrice hallowed by his
spells.

But backward turn—the wondrous shape hath gone!
The round hill towers before thee, smoothly green;
Pass but a few short paces farther on,
Naught but the ragged mountain side is seen.
Thus oft do earthly things delude, I ween,
That in prospective glitter bright and fair,
While time or space or labor intervene.
Approach them, every charm dissolves to air,
Each gorgeous hue hath fled, and all is rude and bare.

And trace yon streamlet down the expanding gorge,
To the famed Basin close beside the way,
Scooped from the rock by its imprisoned surge,
For ages whirling in its foamy spray,

Which, issuing hence, shoots gladly into day,
Till the broad Merrimack it proudly flows,
And into ocean pours a rival sea,
Gladdening fair meadows as it onward goes,
Where, mid the trees, rich towns their heavenward spires
disclose.

And farther down, from Garnsey's lone abode,
By a rude footpath climb the mountain side,
Leaving below the traveller's winding road,
To where the cleft hill yawns abrupt and wide,
As though some earthquake did its mass divide
In olden time; their view the rocky Flume,
Tremendous chasm! rising side by side,
The rocks abrupt wall in the long, high room,
Echoing the wild stream's roar, and dark with vapory
gloom.

But long, too long, I've dwelt as in a dream,
Amid these scenes of high sublimity:
Another pen must eternize the theme
Mine has essayed, though all unworthily.
Franconia! thy wild hills are dear to me,
Would their green woods might be my spirit's home;
Oft o'er the stormy waste of memory
Shall I look back where'er I chance to roam
And see their shining peaks rise o'er its angry foam.

White Mountains, N. H., Old Man of Mountain - Franconia Notch.
Postcard. From the author's collection.

Old Man of the Mountain
Marie A. Hodge

In 1938 The New Hampshire Federation of Women's Clubs published *An Anthology of New Hampshire Poetry*. Marie Hodge was identified as being from Plymouth, New Hampshire.

Old Man of the Mountain,
   of what are you thinking,
As you sit there so solemn
   and still on your throne?
Are you thinking of what mighty
   convulsion of nature
Carved your huge face
   from the solid gray stone?

Are you thinking of time
   in the far distant ages,
Before power of man
   o'er this region held sway,
When, ice-bound and snow-capped,
   this part of creation
In unbroken slumber
   and solitude lay?

Do you think of the wakening
   with one great revulsion,
When Nature's stern law
   had lifted the ban,
And high on the edge
   of the rocky foundation,
Your image appeared
   as a likeness of man?

Could you speak, what strange tales
   of the years that have vanished
You could tell of your mountain
   by man yet untrod,
When you, the rude image
   of Him who created,
Sat silent, communing
   Alone with your God.

The Old Man of the Mountain
Lynn Harold Hough

Privately printed as a small pamphlet for friends and family members, Lynn Harold Hough's *Summer in the White Mountains: 1940*, includes his poem *The Old Man of the Mountain* with allusions to the pending war in Europe. Hough was one of the leading Methodist educators of the twentieth century. Born in Cadiz, Ohio, in 1877 he received his education at Scio College and Drew Theological Seminary, now Drew University. Hough was active in the church and in education. He held pastorates in New Jersey, New York, Brooklyn and Baltimore and at other times in his career was president of Northwestern University and later Dean of Drew Theological Seminary. For his outspoken opposition to the Ku Klux Klan he received an honorary degree from the University of Detroit, a Roman Catholic institution. During the 1960s Hough spent long summers in the White Mountains, first at the Waumbek Hotel in Jefferson and later at the Mount Crescent House in Randolph.

Stone turned into a face,
The swinging arc of a whole mountain
Suddenly lifting a tuft of brow
And peering eye and sharp titanic jaw,
You sweep the valleys with your lofty gaze.
Do you hate what you see? Are you so high
    that you behold
Other valleys where the ugly brown of slowly
    drying blood
Proves man's use only to fertilize the plain?
Do you regret your coming from the stony hill
    in conscious sight?
Do you see some future glory which fills your
    grim face with hope?
I do not know. I only see the lonely quiet of
    your lofty brow,
The hard stern splendor of your stony face.

The Old Man of the Mountain
Charles Fletcher Lummis

A native of Lynn, Massachusetts, Charles Fletcher Lummis was educated at Harvard and then proceeded to explore the American continent from Canada to Chile which he wrote about in several publications including: *A Tramp Across the Continent, Some Strange Corners of Our Country* and several books about Mexico and the Spanish pioneers. Lummis was an editor with the *Los Angeles Times* and later librarian at the Los Angeles Library. Reprinted here are Lummis' two poems that were included in *The White Hills in Poetry*, edited by Eugene R. Musgrove and published in 1912.

Son of the tempest and the earthquake's jars
From out the womb of Chaos wast thou born;
When the first sunrise from the gates of morn
Stepped forth celestial and drew back the bars
Of darkness, and the timorous little stars
Shrank back with Night their mother. Thou hast worn
Millenniums as jewels, and the scars
Gray Time has scratched upon thee but adorn
That pregnant brow with more than kingly grace.
Man's life-tide ebbs and flows as flows the sea:
But thy stout soul, as from thy heavenward place
Thou lookest out upon eternity,
Of passion or of care betrays no trace,
Crowned with a radiant immortality.

Old Man of the Mountains. Franconia Notch. Postcard. From the author's collection.

Sunset on Profile Lake
Charles Fletcher Lumis

The westward sun has left a wake of flame
   Across the silent lake, upon whose breast
The stern, still Face, by wrathful tempests scarred,
   Looks down impassive from the cliffs that frame
The crystal waters as they lie at rest,
   Secure and trustful in his sleepless guard

The regal trout, bestarred with gold and red,
   Shoots headlong high above his native tide
In pure excess of joy, to greet the sun
   Ere yet he seeks his far Pacific bed;
And from the copses on the mountain-side
   The rabbit leaps, a living streak of dun.

Upon the Old Man's brow one lingering ray
   Still clings caressingly, as if God's hand
In radiant benediction rested there;
   And on the breezes' eddying currents, Day
Drifts out beyond the dim horizon strand,
   And Night swims softly down the purple air.

Song of "The Old Man of the Mountain"
Nelson Merrill

Printed for private distribution in 1889, Nelson Merrill's poem, *Song of The Old Man of the Mountain*, was included in a short collection of poetry entitled *Profile Poems* that he had written during his visits in the White Mountains.

LISTEN! Ye Tourists of pleasure,
    While gazing on my face,
A song I'll sing of sweet measure,
    From this my lonely place.

Listen! ye gay young gallants bold,
    And you, ye maidens fair,
Ye gay Flume-Parties, young and old,
    My voice is in the air.

Time was, when I was young like you,
    With fond Companion bless'd
Love only made our union true,
    Nor aught disturb'd our rest.

Long years we pass'd in fond embrace,
    Our granite arms entwin'd,
Our castle walls were firm in place,
    Our mutual bliss enshrin'd.

The Frosts of Time, in a sad year,
  Crept in our mountain home,
And tore from me my darling dear,
  And left me all alone.

Devotion makes my features brave,
  Memory marks my woe,
It comes of watching o'er her grave,
  Down in the vale below.

The Old Man of the Mountain
Fred Cutter Pillsbury

Born in West Newbury, Massachusetts, on April 19, 1857, the Reverend Fred Cutter Pillsbury became a minister in the Methodist Episcopal Church. His poem about the Old Man of the Mountain was included in *The Poets of New Hampshire*, a large anthology of poetry compiled by Bela Chapin and published in 1883.

Above yon threat'ning cloud
   That makes the craggy steeps looks dim,
Mid lightnings fierce and thunders loud
   That hurl their angry spite at him,
Mid summer's heat and winter's snow,
Counting the ages as they come and go,
   Sits the king of New Hampshire hills.

When storms upon the plain
   In fury break, he minds it not;
God sings to him in wind and rain,
   And all his hardships are forgot;
Unvexed by tempest he doth rest
As one in sleep—so still his mighty breast,
   So imperceptible its thrills.

His throne is built so high
   The glittering hosts of light adore;
The bolts of heaven he doth defy;
   Eager, his sceptre o'er and o'er
The sunbeams kiss; his throne the place
Of bright and glittering pearls, the rarest grace
   Alike of morn and paradise.

Tis there Queen Vesper goes
   To shut the golden gates of day,
And give the weary world repose,
   While yet the sun goes on his way,
Glad in his mighty strength, I ween;
And he carries a robe of living green
   For nature's gayest festal guise.

The Old Man of the Mountain
Caroline Anastasia Spalding

Caroline Anastasia Spalding moved to Haverhill, New Hampshire, in 1840 from her hometown of Lyndon, Vermont. The poet was described as "very retiring in her disposition and has ever avoided notoriety." Her poem about the Old Man of the Mountain was included in *The Poets of New Hampshire*, a large anthology of poetry compiled by Bela Chapin and published in 1883.

A scene of rarest beauty,
    Where wood and lake and sky
Were dressed in regal splendor
    Entrancing to the eye.

Our souls had been uplifted
    Above the things of earth,
Its petty cares and triumphs
    Seemed of such trivial worth.

For amid nature's grandeur
    We spent the autumn day;
Through gorge and mountain passes
    We took our wondering way.

And now the lengthening shadows
    The even-tide foretold,
The clouds had added crimson
    To draperies of gold!

We sat in restful silence
   Beside the tranquil lake,
With only woodland voices
   The peaceful calm to break.

The pines were whispering o'er us,
   The mosses fringed the ground,
The ferns and fragrant birches
   Their odors shed around.

But far above us, standing
   Right out against the sky,
A calm, stern face uplifted
   Its granite brow on high.

No trace of mortal weakness,
   Majestic, fearful, grand;
A piece of nature's sculpture
   Carved by the Master's hand.

The whirlwind may encircle
   That rocky, firm retreat,
The winter snows enshroud it,
   The storm in fury beat;

But still unmoved, unyielding,
   Th' impassive face looks down;
No smile the sunbeam wakens,
   The tempest brings no frown.

The thunder peals unheeded,
   The lightnings o'er it flash,
As harmless as the ripples
   Upon the shore that dash!

Oh Thou all-glorious Father!
　Whose hand these wonders piled,
Lifting the mountain masses
　In beauty strangely wild;—

Who, with unerring wisdom,
　Long ages since didst place
Far up among the sunbeams
　This calm, unchanging face,

Give us the strength to conquer
　The ills that crowd our way,
The foes without, the snares within,
　The wiles that lead astray.

To bear unmoved the tempest;
　Fearless and undismayed
To walk beneath the sunshine,
　Remembering it must fade.

Farewell, thou mountain teacher!
　This lesson let us learn,
As in the labyrinth of life
　Our wandering steps return.

He who, with sure foundation,
　A lofty height has won
Need not to fear the whirlwind,
　Nor faint beneath the sun.

The Old Man of the Mountain
John Townsend Trowbridge

In his autobiography John Townsend Trowbridge noted that from the age of twenty he had made his living from writing, of which much was poetry. Born in Ogden, New York, in 1827, Trowbridge described his father's labors as: "He made a clearing, and planted corn and beans and potatoes among the stumps." This simple background provided Trowbridge with no opportunity for a formal education. Later in his life he was given an honorary degree by Dartmouth College. After moving to Boston in 1848 Trowbridge met and worked with the literary community that was centered there. He contributed to the first and many subsequent issues of *The Atlantic* of which he wrote: "I contributed to the early volumes poems, stories, sketches of travel, and one political paper, *We are a Nation*, into which I poured the fervor of my patriotic feelings, on the second election of Lincoln." Trowbridge published over fifty books of poetry and short stories before his death in 1916. His poem *The Old Man of the Mountain* was included in *The White Hills in Poetry* edited by Eugene Musgrove.

All round the lake the wet woods shake
    From drooping boughs their showers of pearl;
From floating skiff to towering cliff
    The rising vapors part and curl.
The west wind stirs among the firs
    High up the mountain side emerging;
The light illumes a thousand plumes
    Through billowy banners round them surging.

A glory smites the craggy heights;
    And in a halo of the haze,
Flushed with faint gold, far up, behold
    That mighty face, that stony gaze!
In the wild sky upborne so high
    Above us perishable creatures,

Confronting Time with those sublime,
  Impassive, adamantine features.

Thou beaked and bald high front, miscalled
  The profile of a human face!
No kin art thou, O Titan brow,
  To puny man's ephemeral race.
The groaning earth to thee gave birth,
  Throes and convulsions of the planet;
Lonely uprose, in grand repose,
  Those eighty feet of facial granite.

Here long, while vast, slow ages passed,
  Thine eyes (if eyes be thine) beheld
But solitudes of crags and woods,
  Where eagles screamed and panthers yelled.
Before the fires of our pale sires
  In the first log-built cabin twinkled,
Or red men came for fish and game,
  That scalp was scarred, that face was wrinkled.

We may not know how long ago
  That ancient countenance was young;
Thy sovereign brow was seamed as now
  When Moses wrote and Homer sung.
Empires and states it antedates,
  And wars, and arts, and crime, and glory;
In that dim morn when Christ was born
  Thy head with centuries was hoary.

Thou lonely one! nor frost, nor sun,
  Nor tempest leaves on thee its trace;
The stormy years are but as tears
  That pass from thy unchanging face.
With unconcern as grand and stern,
  Those features viewed, which now survey us,
A green world rise from seas of ice,
  And order come from mud and chaos.

Canst thou not tell what then befell?
　　What forces moved, or fast or slow;
How grew the hills; what heats, what chills,
　　What strange, dim life, so long ago?
High-visaged peak, wilt thou not speak?
　　One word, for all our learned wrangle!
What earthquakes shaped, what glaciers scraped,
　　That nose, and gave the chin its angle?

Our pygmy thought to thee is naught,
　　Our petty questionings are vain;
In its great trance thy countenance
　　Knows not compassion nor disdain.
With far-off hum we go and come,
　　The gay, the grave, the busy-idle
And all things done to thee are one,
　　Alike the burial and the bridal.

Thy permanence, long ages hence,
　　Will mock the pride of mortals still.
Returning springs, with songs and wings
　　And fragrance, shall these valleys fill;
And free winds blow, fall rain or snow,
　　The mountains brim their crystal beakers;
Still come and go, still ebb and flow,
　　The summer tides of pleasure-seekers:

The dawns shall gild the peaks where build
　　The eagles, many a future pair;
The gray scud lag on wood and crag,
　　Dissolving in the purple air;
The sunlight gleam on lake and stream,
　　Boughs wave, storms break, and still at even
All glorious hues the world suffuse,
　　Heaven mantle earth, earth melt in heaven!

Nations shall pass like summer's grass,
　　And times unborn grow old and change;

New governments and great events
   Shall rise, and science new and strange;
Yet will thy gaze confront the days
   With its eternal calm and patience,
The evening red still light thy head,
   Above thee burn the constellations.

O silent speech, that well can teach
   The little worth of words or fame!
I go my way, but thou wilt stay
   While future millions pass the same:
But what is this I seem to miss?
   Those features fall into confusion!
A further pace—where was that face?
   The veriest fugitive illusion!

Gray eidolon! so quickly gone,
   When eyes, that make thee, onward move;
Whose vast pretence of permanence
   A little progress can disprove!
Like some huge wraith of human faith
   That to the mind takes form and measure;
Grim monolith of creed or myth,
   Outlined against the eternal azure!

O Titan, how dislimned art thou!
   A withered cliff is all we see;
That giant nose, that grand repose,
   Have in a moment ceased to be;
Or still depend on lines that blend,
   On merging shapes, and sight, and distance,
And in the mind alone can find
   Imaginary brief existence!

Final Words

Three Impressions

Epilogue

THREE IMPRESSIONS

The Homes of The New World: Impressions of America
Fredrika Bremer

A 19th-century Swedish novelist, Fredrika Bremer once spent two years traveling in America. In August 1851, just before returning to Sweden, she visited the White Mountains where she stayed in the Lafayette House, very near the Old Man of the Mountain. During her two year trip, Bremer had often written home to her sister about her trip and life in America. In 1853 these letters were published as a book, *The Homes of The New World: Impressions of America*, from which the following passage is quoted:

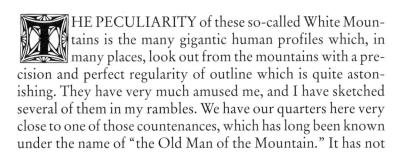

THE PECULIARITY of these so-called White Mountains is the many gigantic human profiles which, in many places, look out from the mountains with a precision and perfect regularity of outline which is quite astonishing. They have very much amused me, and I have sketched several of them in my rambles. We have our quarters here very close to one of those countenances, which has long been known under the name of "the Old Man of the Mountain." It has not any nobility in its features, but resembles a very old man in a bad humor, and with a nightcap on his head, who is looking out from the mountain half inquisitive. Far below the old giant's face is an enchanting little lake, resembling a bright oval toilet-glass, enclosed in a verdant frame of leafage. The Old Man of the Mountain looks out gloomily over this quiet lake, and the clouds float far below his chin.

A Presidential Address
Dwight David Eisenhower

On June 24, 1955, Dwight David Eisenhower, the 34th President of the United States, spoke in Franconia Notch at the celebrations commemorating the 150th anniversary of the discovery of the Old Man of the Mountain. Other Presidents known to have visited Franconia Notch are: Andrew Jackson, Calvin Coolidge, Grover Cleveland, Franklin Pierce, and Ulysees Grant.

Only a few moments ago, I had the first opportunity of my life to look a the Old Man of the Mountain. The natural question asked me was, "What did you think of it, Mr. President?" I answered, as anyone would in polite conversation, and said, "Remarkable. Wonderful. Interesting."

The real thought that crossed my mind was: what does the Old Man of the Mountain think of us?

He has been there through time. In his lonely vigil up at the top of that mountain—let us not try to go back to what he may have been thinking through those ages before our civilization first discovered him—150 years ago he saw great ox carts going through these roads where now we travel in an instant. He saw the fastest means of transportation—the horse. Finally he saw stage coaches. He saw only here and there a habitation, a sparsely settled wilderness.

He has seen mankind go from the sailing ship and from the horse and buggy to the jet airplane and the ability to cross the ocean in a few hours. He has seen the great sciences of radio and television come to us. He has seen every American have, with his morning breakfast, the day's news of the world. He has seen the great electronics industry—electric lights, telephones and telegraphy, and all the things by which we live today. All of these changes have come about.

But can you believe, as he stands up there, almost in infinite majesty, that he thinks it is of great concern that we travel at a rate that multiplies the speed of our forefathers?

I believe he thinks of something deeper than that. Possibly he recalls the words with which our Forefathers started the greatest of all human documents: "When in the course of human events it becomes necessary for one people to dissolve the political bands which have connected them with another, and assume among the powers of the earth that separate and equal status to which both the laws of nature and nature's God intended them, a decent respect for the opinions of mankind impel them to declare the reasons which have led to their separation. We hold these truths to be self-evident, that all men are created equal, that they are endowed by their Creator with certain unalienable rights. Among these are life, liberty, and the pursuit of happiness."

These immortal words must mean a great deal to the Old Man of the Mountain. He must contemplate them from time to time. I think we—with him—understand life. We know the instinct of self-preservation, and we know what living means to us, in our separate capacities, in our separate areas. We know what liberty is: the individual right to do as we please as long as we do not infringe upon similar rights of others.

But the pursuit of happiness—he must have noted that those writers did not create this government to give us happiness. Far better they knew than to try to define happiness for any one of us—the pursuit of happiness in liberty each according to his own desires, to the deepest aspirations of his own soul.

Now, what have we done about it? Where do we find happiness?

Possibly that is what he is wondering today.

We know certain things. We know we would like to be at peace. We do not want to send our boys off into the Armed Services to serve in foreign lands. We do not want to dwell in fear. We do not want to contemplate the horrible things that could happen to us in a new war.

At home, we want to live comfortably. We want to be well-informed. We want to have neighbors around us that we like.

But as we pursue happiness, are we thinking only of these material things? Then how do we attain it?

If we attain money to do certain things, then we want more money. If we attain a high office, we want a higher one. If there is no higher one, we would like to invent it. We always want something more.

Now, what is there more? Maybe the "more" is to try to discover what others around us find as their idea of the pursuit of happiness, what it is that mankind wants, instead of each of us separately. Can we integrate the desires, the aspirations, the hopes of our community, and then do our part to achieve that?

In so doing, I wonder whether the Old Man wouldn't approve of us more than he may at present. Because he well knows, if he has watched us, that each individual is made up of two sets of qualities. One we call the noble: courage, readiness to sacrifice, love for our families, respect for others.

And he knows also those other qualities, of selfishness and greed and ambition, and things that set men one against the other, and nations one against the other. He recognizes the right of a group, whether it be community, or whether it be nation, to protect itself, to make certain of its own security. But certainly he must applaud every effort we make to understand others, whether it be individuals, or cities, or States or nations, to understand others as we understand ourselves, and in this way bring somewhat closer, each by his own efforts, that great dream of mankind: a peaceful world in which each of us may continue to develop.

Whether we do it through church, or through our schools, through any kind of community enterprise, through the family, through our own reading, we do not seek knowledge for itself. We do not seek acquaintanceship with the classics merely that we may quote a line from it.

We seek the knowledge and the thinking of the past that we may bring it together—here today—and help forward, each in his own little fashion, that great progress that I am certain the Old Man of the Mountain yet hopes that mankind will achieve: that objective of peace on earth, goodwill to men.

I would not for a moment leave this stand with the thought that we may have these things merely by thinking, or hoping, or wishing. But behind every effort there must be an aspiration, there must be a devotion to a cause.

If we are sufficiently devoted to the cause of peace, to the kind of progress of which I speak, we will be strong, and then we will be able to cooperate with others, because only strength can cooperate—weakness cannot cooperate, it can only beg; we will be able to cooperate and to help lead the world toward that promised goal.

So I would say our best birthday present to the Old Man of the Mountain is that we make up our minds, each in his own fashion, to do his part in bringing about that hope for mankind that the Old Man must have.

Thank you a lot. It has been a great pleasure to meet you all. Goodbye.

THE OLD MAN OF THE MOUNTAIN.

The Old Man of the Mountain. From *Gems of American Scenery: White Mountains* by Albert Bierstadt. New York, 1875. The photographs in Bierstadt's book were taken in 1860 and may be the earliest photographs of the White Mountains. From the author's collection.

"God Almighty Has Hung Out a Sign..."
Daniel Webster

Born on January 18, 1782 in Salisbury, New Hampshire, and educated at Dartmouth College, Daniel Webster would become one of Americas most eminent Constitutional lawyers. Lawyer, orator, Congressman, Senator, and Secretary of State, Webster described the American Constitution as "undoubtedly the greatest approximation toward human perfection the political world ever yet experienced... which, perhaps, will forever stand in the history of mankind, without a parallel." Of the Old Man of the Mountain, the emblem of his native state, he said:

MEN HANG OUT their signs indicative of their respective trades. Shoemakers hang out a gigantic shoe; jewelers, a monster watch; even the dentist hangs out a gold tooth; but up in the Franconia Mountains God Almighty has hung out a sign to show that in New England He makes men.

EPILOGUE

Epilogue

 Y DEFINITION an epilogue is the concluding section of a book where the author completes the whole plan of the work. You, the reader, must now do that. You must now add to the literature that has been written about The Old Man of the Mountains. Remember your first visit to Franconia Notch, your first sight of the Old Man, a hike up Cannon Mountain to the ledges, a ride on the tramway, visits to Profile Lake, Echo Lake or Lonesome Lake or a day of skiing in the company of the Old Man. Write a story, write a poem, or be artistic and draw a picture. Let there be no restrictions imposed on your imagination. (The editor sincerely regrets that he will not be able to read all of these wonderful pieces.) Have fun and good luck.